JOURNEY TO MOUNT ATHOS

FATHER SPYRIDON BAILEY

Published in 2014 by FeedARead.com Publishing
– Arts Council funded.

A CIP catalogue record for this title is available
from the British Library.

To Stephanie – *the reason for my return journey*

"Someone who bears a grudge while he prays is like a person who sows in the sea and expects to reap a harvest."

- Saint Isaac the Syrian.

Chapter One

The sea and sky were a match of uninterrupted blue: flat as glass and a colour I had never before seen outside of Hollywood movies. The ferry chugged ahead quickly enough to leave a thick white trail that stretched out behind us. It had a flat deck long enough for three vans in line, and at the rear was a three-storey structure on top of which I now sat.

There were about fifty of us spread out on rows of plastic chairs which were bolted to iron fixings, all covered by a large roof held aloft by posts but with no walls. This meant there was plenty of shade, and even by ten in the morning it was needed, even as a cool breeze blew off the water and across the assembled pilgrims. Most of the crowd were Greek, but amongst the conversations it was possible to detect the odd French voice. I couldn't hear any English, and I wouldn't hear a woman's voice again until I returned to the world.

I was travelling alone and felt free to sit and bask in the scene. As the ferry left the small town of Ouranoupolis a couple of monks climbed to the top of the stairs to the upper platform and found themselves seats. I was excited to see them, as their long grey beards were buffeted over their scruffy rassas. They looked exactly as the countless books I had read about Athos had led me to expect. Their presence somehow made what I was doing more real and yet a part of me still couldn't believe I was finally going to be there.

A flock of gulls began to circle the ship and a few of the passengers moved out from under the shade in order to throw bread to them. As the gulls recognised the source of the food they began circling closer to us until something magical occurred. Their air speed and that of the ferry matched perfectly and the gulls hung above us as though motionless. More of the pilgrims moved to feed them; they threw bread directly to the open mouths above them and began to laugh as the birds hungrily swallowed their offerings. A moustached Greek man was the first to hold his arm aloft clutching a crust. At first the gulls seemed nervous, but after a few successful feeds they moved close enough to simply take the food from the man's hands. Other men began to copy him until the gulls were feeding inches from the men's reach. Cameras around me began clicking and everyone grinned like schoolboys at the spectacle. As the ferry pulled further away from land the winds changed and the seagulls returned to their circling before drifting away from us. The event seemed to relax everyone; smiles and laughter were everywhere as conversations began to spring up around me.

I began to think about why I had made the trip. It had been an ambition for a couple of decades, but the urge to fulfil it had become more pressing in the past twelve months. I had an urgent question that I needed answering, and I hoped to find a wise monk to help me resolve it (I could pretend otherwise, but that's the way it was). In fact it wasn't so much a question as a sense of anger about something that had been bothering me for some time and from which I felt unable to free myself. The anger had become directed at a particular person and I was becoming increasingly uncomfortable with feeling this way. I had prayed long and hard, but there seemed no solution making itself known. So a big part of my motivation for going to Athos was to find a way to deal with my feelings. As I sat on the ferry I once again began to think through the issues when all at once I knew what to do. It was ridiculous. I thought I was going to Athos because of this one particular thing, and as we sailed towards the peninsula the solution was obvious. I had an overwhelming sense of the other person's holiness, I understood completely their true identity as a child of God, and as this realisation dawned on me, it became impossible to cling to the feelings of anger. I was filled with relief and a realisation that the reason I thought I was making the pilgrimage was no longer true. I was now unencumbered by these previous expectations and was open to simply experience what was to come for what it was. It was enormously freeing and though I couldn't have articulated it, I sensed God's hand on the whole situation. I was wary of attaching too much to this, but it intensified further my sense of expectation for the trip.

As I was processing what was happening the first of the monasteries came into sight. We had been sailing for about forty minutes and it seemed that from nowhere a low three-storey building emerged, made of white stone, sitting at the very edge of the sea. A number of the passengers moved to where they could take photographs, which pleased me because I realised I wasn't the only one aboard getting excited at what was happening.

The ferry eased alongside a small concrete jetty and a few figures jumped to dry land. Almost immediately we were off again and I watched as the pilgrims we had left ashore walked towards and then disappeared into the still, ancient structure that seemed to sit waiting for them. The outer walls seemed to wrap protectively around the life that they held, a protective shield for the monks who laboured within.

This pattern of first seeing and then pulling up to monasteries was repeated five more times. Some of the coastline monasteries were clearly Greek with their blue, domed churches nestling among the beautiful buildings around them. One huge complex however, stood out as Russian. It was vast. Four-storey buildings sitting beside towers and onion domes and roofs of red and blue slate that were startling in their intensity. It was a reminder of the universal importance of Athos, that it wasn't just a Greek thing, but that for all Orthodox around the world this was a spiritual centre; the heart beating in a body of prayer spoken in every language.

As we caught sight of one monastery I noticed a number of half built sections but could see that it wasn't new.

"Why is it only half built?" I asked the Greek chap beside me.

In reasonable English he said "They started it before the Russian revolution, but when the communists took power, they cut off the money and also the monks. So it has stood like that ever since." He smiled at the story, and I nodded my thanks as I took in what I was seeing.

I noticed a small monk who looked to be in his seventies lifting his bag onto a flat surface a few metres away from the passengers and he proceeded to roll it out to reveal a collection of prayer ropes and other small items. At first no one responded, but then after one man began fingering the various objects on display, a few others became curious and joined him. Within a few minutes the monk had half a dozen customers and was making a good number of sales. I was curious myself, but my English reserve kept me in my seat.

Soon a voice announced through a small speaker that we were approaching Daphne. This was my stop. I looked out ahead of us to see five or six orange roofed buildings, all no more than two storeys high. My sense of anticipation was immense; the dark green bushes ahead of us were cut through by white dusty paths that led off to everything I had been dreaming about for a long time. This was the Holy Mountain, the place of saints and hermits; it didn't seem possible that I was really here.

Most of the passengers were going ashore at Daphne, and queues began to form down the stairways and along the deck to the bow. Immediately in front of me a young Russian priest turned and addressed me in Greek. I smiled, and said

"I'm sorry, I'm English." This was a phrase I would become accustomed to repeating. He looked with surprise at me as I was dressed as a Greek priest.

"English?" He repeated back at me in a thick accent.

"Yes ," I confirmed, amused at his reaction.

"And a priest?" He continued, arching his eyebrows. Again I confirmed it, and finally he said "Orthodox?" At this last enquiry I smiled, even more than acknowledging I was a priest; to be Orthodox meant everything to me. He pursed his lips slightly, "I did not know there were English Orthodox." His dark brown eyes looked intently at me.

"Yes, many," I assured him, "the Church is growing quickly in the west." He nodded approval at this and we moved forward with the line of pilgrims to set foot on holy ground. We smiled our goodbyes but would meet again soon.

I had indeed flown in from England to a place and culture unlike anything I had previously known. But my journey to Mount Athos had in truth started many years before.

"Do not be always wanting everything to turn out as you think it should, but rather as God pleases, then you will be undisturbed and thankful in prayer."

- Saint Nilus

Chapter Two

In 1965 Shrewsbury was a lot further from Mount Athos than it is today: further in every possible way. Religious life in Britain was in decline, but generally people still held on to certain attitudes and customs that could be called Christian. The BBC had not yet turned its back on Christianity, let alone begun its all-out assault on Christian values. It was a time of change; the year The Rolling Stones released Satisfaction, the year of my birth. I entered a culture where people were rejecting traditions and authorities and simply losing interest in what the Church of England had to say.

My parents had been married in a Baptist chapel, I was baptised (or christened as it was called by non-churchgoers) by the local Anglican minister, and at around the age of five I was sent to a Methodist Sunday school. I resented this intrusion on my weekend, we lived in a rural area and Sundays to me were a time for playing for hours in the fields around our street. I remember a sense of real freedom in my childhood, something too few children today are able to enjoy. The Methodist chapel hadn't been chosen because of any kind of theological leaning, it was the nearest one and to most people it didn't really make a lot of difference. One denomination was seen as pretty much like another, as long as the vicar or minister was "nice" and they didn't get up to anything odd, then no one objected. I suspect the enthusiastic Methodist lady who lived two doors down from us and who had a daughter in my class at school also had some influence on the decision to rob me of my free weekend hours.

Looking back I wonder how many seeds were sown and how grateful I should be for that brief Christian influence in my life. I have no memory of ever being impressed or enthused by anything that happened there; in fact I distinctly recall being bored and wanting to be elsewhere. They had a deep blue carpet that was kept immaculately clean which always made me feel uneasy, as though mucky kids should watch their steps here. And I was as mucky as they came. The only other thing I can recall was a painting of Jesus that left a real impression on me. He was portrayed rather sentimentally, and rather fair-skinned, but the painter had captured a sense of another land, a hot place from some distant past. It was the only religious image I think I ever saw outside of a book during those years, and I distinctly remember thinking that I liked this man. Nothing more than that, but it may have been enough.

After that brief attempt to raise me with some Christian influence, my parents gave in to my pleadings and after a short while I was excused Sunday school forever. I resumed my habits of climbing trees and disappearing for hours into the woods and that was as much church as I was exposed to for the next fourteen years.

The journey that resulted in me setting foot on Athos really had two early stages. The first was discovering the Christian faith and then the second was the call of Orthodoxy. I have few important memories of my early childhood, but I do recall sitting on a hill with friends at the age of about eight or nine. We were discussing why we couldn't see God, or more specifically why He didn't reveal Himself to us. All kinds of possible answers were suggested, such as the fact that none of us closed our eyes when prayers were said in school assemblies. It is only through this memory that I realise that though there was no subject called Religious Education as they have in schools today, there was an attempt being made to give us some kind of awareness of the faith. Someone within our school system was at least trying to reach the heathen.

The other memory I have of that conversation is that I realised at that age that I didn't know if God existed or not. But I remember very clearly thinking that if I ever believed in Him I would have to devote my entire life to Him. At that time I could only understand this in one way, and the thought of becoming a monk frightened me. I don't recall where I had seen or heard of monasticism, but it genuinely made me afraid. I had no idea of serving God in the world or even the priesthood. This may sound unlikely, but it is very clear in my mind how I understood with absolute certainty that faith would demand a response that would affect the whole of life, that to know that God was there would not be something that could be tucked away in the back of the mind or given a small portion of the week. Remembering this today has always motivated me not to underestimate the perception of even young children when it comes to grasping the consequences of faith. People often dismiss the way children see things in black and white, a worldview unclouded by the grey areas of adult compromise. And though I know many people will see it as naïve, I still believe things are very simple and obvious in that way, at least when it comes to day-to-day living. Too often we like to avoid the straightforward in favour of uncertainty because we are looking for a way to excuse ourselves from the demands of truth. Too often compromise is really a way of following our own wishes without feeling guilty about it. But I still believe that so long as we keep listening to our conscience, things remain simple, and we know in our hearts when we are trying to justify what we want over the revealed will of God.

So the first stage of my journey was a slow one. I eventually lost the desire to know if God was there and replaced it with an all-out rejection of the possibility that He could exist. Like many teenagers I became preoccupied with the pressures of school and fitting in with my peers and at high school I was isolated from any kind of Christian teaching. We had a social development tutor who arranged discussions once each week on issues such as sexuality and various sociological topics. We considered this as nothing more than an hour off from our studies and never took him seriously. On one occasion he arranged for his Indian guru to come and talk to us. A small dark man accompanied by two attractive western women sat in front us, and he proceeded to impart his wisdom. He shared insights such as never eat before brushing your teeth in the morning that we reacted to by sniggering, much to the annoyance of our teacher. The whole thing was a joke to us, thankfully, and we never saw the guru again. The episode struck us as funny at the time but later in life I realised how easy it is for teachers to have an input into our children's consciousness that we often know nothing about. I certainly never went home to tell my parents about the experience. I subsequently made a conscious decision to enquire about the lessons my children received, especially in Religious Education.

In my early teens I had no interest of any kind in religious questions; I was utterly immersed in the human world around me and the humanistic interpretations of our life on the planet. And in this state I went off as an undergraduate to study for my degree. Only with hindsight am I able to recognise the thread running through what happened to me in the following years. God's hand reached out and held me, guided me and blessed me.

It started when I met a young woman from Ireland. She was a devout Roman Catholic and was clearly intent on sharing something with me: I am sure she would have been praying for me but I was simply interested in a pretty face. I agreed to join her to the local church for evening mass, just because I was happy to be around her. At the door she blessed herself with holy water from the stoup and laughing she threw a handful over me. She managed to do it in a way that made me think she was just being playful, but little did I understand her true motive. The service itself was impenetrable to me, I watched a man doing and saying things, and none of it went any further than that. I never imagined that there could be any kind of reality beyond the outward actions; I really was dead to any form of spiritual truth.

My intention had been to study English so as to become a teacher. The course required us to pick other subjects to fill in the timetable and after tasting the first year's lectures I decided to go for philosophy. By the end of the second year I dropped all other subjects and focussed entirely on philosophy. I spent my days wrestling with the issues we were studying, and found myself engaging with them way beyond the world of academia. We studied metaphysics, ethics, philosophy of the mind and politics. We moved from the Greeks through to early twentieth century thinkers, but it always stopped short of one ultimate question. This was a philosophy course and so devoid of any mention of that certain three letter word: only when I later studied a degree in theology did I discover that these same writers had indeed been concerned with God's existence. I became consumed with the issues that the course raised and for the first time in my life it mattered to me whether I was just a highly developed animal or if there could be something more to man. I began to have the clichéd late night student conversations with friends and found myself walking to lectures with arguments and questions rolling around in my mind.

It came to a head when I found myself at home for the summer holidays. I needed to know if God was there, and I prayed. I prayed with a desperation and need that was overwhelming, and as I spoke aloud to a God I didn't yet know, He touched me. At once I sensed that I wasn't alone, that He was there and always had been. I sensed God's presence in a tangible and unexpected way that shook me and shook my whole understanding of life and the world. The sense of His presence was momentary, but it was enough. It would take time for that sense of God to grow stronger, and there would be many hours of struggling with what it meant, but I had experienced something that was beyond the rational mind. An aspect of the Christian faith that many who don't share it fail to understand is that belief in God is not just an intellectual pursuit.

Christians do not have faith because they have simply decided to agree in their mind with a particular set of doctrines or to satisfy some psychological need. Christian faith is based in the living experience of God here, in this life. It was a real shock for me to realise this, that the words and actions I had been dismissing were only the surface of something much deeper. This was not a conversion, only a glimpse, I had been touched by God but there was still a long way to go.

I returned to the epicurean world of college with a new understanding of myself and life. But I was soon to discover that the one form of religion unacceptable amongst alternative people is Christianity. I could have declared myself a Buddhist or a Hare Krishna, and all would have been "cool", but the Christian religion carried with it images of Stars On Sunday and blue-rinsed ladies peering over horn-rimmed spectacles into Victorian hymn books. Not cool at all. But for me Christ had nothing to do with any of that, I had no connection with any of the cultural trappings that my friends were rejecting. One further blessing at this time was the discovery that hidden away in my circle of friends there was a young woman who I didn't really know very well, but who I discovered shared the Christian faith. She later became my wife.

During the final year of my studies I read a few books, tried to pray, and considered the ramifications of what being a Christian meant. The first realisation was that I had to join other Christians in worship. I dreaded this. I had long, dishevelled hair and couldn't imagine being welcomed into any decent middle class church. During one of the holidays I walked down to the same Methodist chapel I had escaped from as a child, and braced myself for the reaction I expected to receive. It wasn't middle class, but it was as respectable as anywhere on earth. There were about a dozen people scattered around the yellow pews, none of them below retirement age. The service was rather lifeless and uninspiring, but I tried to make the words of the hymns and prayers my own. After the service I headed towards the exit hoping to slip away, and it was then that I discovered something wonderful. The old faces looking back at me remembered me from Sunday school; they greeted me with the joy of a father welcoming home his lost son. In the warmth of their welcome I realised that beyond the ancient suits and greying hair, there was the same God who had touched me when I had first prayed to him. I understood that the preconceptions and prejudices had all been mine and that here was a group of people who had been exposed to the same God as I was seeking to find more of. This was something of a revelation to me, and for a while I always made a point of joining them whenever I was at home.

After my degree I ended up living in Bath for six months. I discovered an Anglican parish populated with a large number of people around my own age, and it seemed as good a place as any to live. The parish congregation was split into the traditional Anglicans who used the main body of the church building, and this other group who the vicar allowed to meet in a large room for more informal worship. This division should have rung alarm bells in my head but I was oblivious to what it might mean. The alternative group had guitars and inspirational speakers. They exhibited what they identified as gifts of the Spirit, and there were regular healings and prophecies made. Around me I would hear people speaking in tongues and hands would be raised in an exhibition of emotion. The whole dynamic was very powerful and would carry everyone along: I hated it. The hymns sounded like children's verse, they lacked any spiritual or theological depth, and the leaders of worship were treated like rock stars. There was an expectation that if someone was a Christian they would automatically be given great spiritual powers and gifts. At this point I couldn't have articulated why it was wrong, but something deep inside me told me to flee. However, I was living in a room hired from one of the church leaders and felt I couldn't throw his hospitality back in his face.

The thread of God's will continued to make itself known in my life. While struggling with how uncomfortable I was in this situation I read a poster advertising a talk being given in the Anglican church hall by the local Russian Orthodox priest. He was to speak about something called the Jesus Prayer. I hadn't heard of this before but was interested enough to go along. This was really what started the second stage of my journey; the talk would plant another seed deep into my soul.

"Saint Agatho was accused by certain people of various sins and he replied each time "I am a sinner". But when they said to him "Agatho is a heretic" he objected. When they asked him why he had suffered all the accusations with patience but did not endure this last one, he replied "Those sins are inherent in a man, and we hope to receive forgiveness of them through the mercy of God, but a heretic is separated from God. Remember, no one is sinless except God, it is inherent in every person, even if his life be but a single day. But when it comes to the truth of faith this is a different matter.""

Chapter Three

The meeting was well attended, a mixture of curious Anglicans and representatives of the Orthodox parish who no doubt came as much to support their priest as to hear the talk. He was a very serious looking man; I didn't see a smile touch his lips all night. He had a full grey beard and in his black clothing he looked like he meant business. I don't remember much of what he said, except that he gave a warning to anyone thinking of saying the Jesus Prayer to only do so under the guidance of a spiritual father or director (aimed I assumed at the Anglicans in the room). I ignored this warning and began using the Jesus Prayer as part of my daily routine. The words "Lord Jesus Christ, Son of God have mercy on me a sinner" seemed to first rise up to heaven before then coming back to earth in the second section. This rhythm of ascent and descent felt natural and comfortable to me immediately, it didn't require any artificial emotion or use of imagination, but kept the mind and heart focussed on God.

At the end of the lecture an invitation was extended for anyone interested to join the Orthodox parish on its pilgrimage to a local disused church for a service. After expressing an interest a lift was offered and I gladly accepted. The Orthodox parishioners were friendly but struck me as slightly wary of us Anglicans. I sensed from their conversation that they didn't see themselves as just another denomination among many. I was intrigued to know more and spent the next week or so thinking about the encounter with them.

The disused church turned out to be an ancient site with little more than crumbling walls and no roof. They had set up a makeshift altar with a line of icons and candles in front of it. At first I felt more of a tourist than a participator in the service, but slowly I became absorbed in what was happening. The service was in Russian, which meant I couldn't understand a word of what was being sung, but ironically I felt a much deeper connection with the mood and tone than anything I had experienced in Christian worship before. It was as though the Liturgy was expressing something far deeper and more substantial than any folk hymn strummed on an acoustic guitar had ever managed. But it wasn't just a style of worship that I was responding to; the people themselves expressed something profound in their demeanour and actions. As they made the sign of the cross over themselves it was tangible how real it was to them, that they truly believed in the blessing that this action evoked. There was a bishop present, and everyone treated him with enormous respect and honour. Like the priest, his presence was one of dignity and dare I say it: holiness.

After the Liturgy we headed back to one of the men's homes for coffee and I was introduced for the first time to a man who would have an enormous impact on my life. He was a monk visiting Bath on his journey from Mount Athos to mid-Wales where he was going to join another monk at a hermitage. I was drawn to his humility and gentleness, which hid a sharp wit and intelligence. In a brief conversation he explained the peninsula of Mount Athos to me, and I wondered how he could ever have brought himself to leave. I met him just a couple more times at Sunday Liturgies which I occasionally attended, and then he was gone.

After a while my contract came to an end at the pottery where I was working and I decided to move to Sheffield. My fiancée was living up there and we had managed to get through a year of only seeing each other every ten weeks or so. I had made and glazed a couple of three bar crosses while in Bath, and they would hang in every flat and house I would live in for the next twenty-five years. But for now I let thoughts of Orthodoxy drift from my mind. I had no understanding of ecclesiology, I considered an individual personal faith sufficient to establish membership of the Church, and ideas of who or what the Church might actually be were utterly alien to me. So I let Orthodoxy be pushed out of my thinking, or at least settle somewhere in the shadows of my consciousness. I had come to the conclusion that God wanted me to serve as a priest, and so sure was I of the inevitability of this I gave no further thought to career or advancement. I was happy to find whatever kind of work would suit the moment, because I knew where I was headed – at least I thought I did.

Eventually I ended up working for the Church of England under the title of Pastoral Assistant. This consisted of making visits to the elderly, attending and even leading house study groups, and delivering sermons. Without any kind of theological training I was allowed to stand in church and tell the congregation how I saw things. Some of them had been attending church for fifty or sixty years and here was I only twenty-four years old, having been a Christian barely three years, expounding on the gospel for them. Unbelievably all went well and I was sent off to meet the Director of Ordinands for the diocese in order to test out my claim to a religious calling. At the time he seemed very thorough, he interviewed me each Wednesday afternoon for about ten weeks before agreeing to send me off to a bishop's selection conference. As I look back now I realise that such a decision based on only ten hours of conversation is quite a gamble; and he was considered to be more thorough than many in other dioceses.

The Church of England chooses its ministers using the same system as the army selects its officers. They send a group of chaps (mainly men at that time) to a remote conference centre or stately home, and run them through a few interviews and group debates to test them out. Mine was pretty uneventful and once I had been given the green light it was time to choose a theological college. I first visited The College of the Resurrection in Mirfield. This was an Anglican monastery that prepared young men for ministry. I was attracted to the way of life there, but before leaving I got talking to one of the students in his room. He described the sense of isolation his wife was enduring, and how the regime was really only suited to single men. Whether he was right or just one man going through a hard time, it was enough of a warning to send me looking elsewhere. I eventually settled on Lincoln Theological College because by this time I was married and I was impressed with the family atmosphere.

The three years of study were a mixture of real highs and lows. I was surprised at how often I had to argue the case for even the most fundamental of Christian doctrines. Resurrection and Christ's full divinity weren't even on the horizon of many of the students' thinking. In seminars I found myself having to defend even the belief that God was personal: I was accused by someone preparing for ordination that such notions were just anthropomorphism gone wild. Even many of the lecturers expressed open amusement at the simple beliefs of the "ordinary" people in the pews. There was a liberal bias to much of the biblical interpretation and I wondered how my peers would manage to hide their real beliefs once they were standing in their pulpits.

These were certainly some of the lows, but I am grateful too for the opportunity those three years gave me to study the Fathers and Church history. Even before I was ordained in the Church of England I was beginning to recognise the absurd situation in which we as Protestants found ourselves. I was convinced that there is not only objective truth in the universe, but that the living Truth has made Himself known to us in the incarnation. I was therefore faced with the question of which of the competing claims that the many denominations made about their version of truth could be right. It was simple. Either one of them was right or none of them were right. Lincoln trained Methodist ministers alongside the Anglicans and it quickly became apparent that the two groups believed very different things about the Eucharist. This is just one example of divergence. Of course, it is possible to retreat to the position where one says that none of these issues are central to the faith, and that so long as we share the essentials, then we are all part of one Church. But this wasn't a satisfactory answer; I knew that if the Church taught falsely on these things, then nothing could be believed. Christ Himself assured the Church that it would not be defeated by the attacks of Satan. If there was truth then it had to still be somewhere, maintained and protected from the time of Christ and the Apostles.

At the weekend retreat before my ordination I began to seriously question how the Church of England, which had only been in existence for a few hundred years, could really be the Church that had nurtured the true faith for two thousand years. And yet I felt convinced that God had called me to the priesthood. And so, with this conflict gnawing away at me, I knelt before the Bishop of Sheffield and entered the ranks of the Anglican clergy. I wanted to believe that this really was the Church, within which my children were going to be nurtured on the ancient faith of the fathers; nothing would have made me happier than to find a way to resolve my issues and allow me to accept the Anglican faith. So I had my own questions that wouldn't be expressed from the pulpit too.

As an ordained clergyman I began a curacy in a large ex-mining town to the North of Sheffield. A parish of twenty-three thousand souls with a regular Sunday congregation of about sixty people. But with so many ex-miners in the town the undertakers called at least twice a week: I officiated at an average of over a hundred and forty funerals a year for the four years I was there. Surprisingly this was the most valuable part of my ministry. I was constantly facing death and bereavement, the graveyard was ridiculously familiar to me, and every street I drove or walked along seemed to have at least one house where I had heard people pour out their grief. The experience confronted me with the reality of death in a way that no book or movie could ever manage. The absolute reality of our mortality was driven into me and has never left me. The brevity of our time on earth is a precious realisation. It puts speed to our feet and frees us from the fear that this world can ever lay claim to us. Whenever anxieties about money or the future would creep into me, I would drive them away with the reassuring comfort that this life is shorter than we can ever know. Staring into hundreds of open graves really does put a healthy dose of perspective on the petty things we too often get worked up about.

During the second year of my curacy I discovered an Orthodox book service and began ordering the odd volume. The first was "Contemporary Ascetics of Mount Athos" which remains one of my favourite books to go back to. The more I read the more the questions about authority and ecclesiology grew. I was invited to present a talk as part of the cathedral training programme for new clergy on Orthodox spirituality: I don't recall ever showing my hand so early on but the fact that they did this clearly shows that someone had heard me talking about this stuff. It was more difficult to deal with these issues now because I had been entrusted with the care of many devout Christian people. I felt as though I was misleading the congregation by keeping quiet about what I was thinking, but I also had doubts about whether I could trust where these thoughts were leading.

During that time I was made an offer by a travel firm to visit the Holy Land at a price I couldn't turn down. The hope was that clergy would then use their company to take parties from their parishes on future trips. It was an incredible experience in many ways. One day near Bethlehem one of the party asked the tour guide why the Orthodox had churches at all the main sites. He smiled and said, "Because they were here first." That moment reinforced everything I had been thinking, and as we made our way towards Nazareth I knew I was approaching an important decision in my life.

One evening back in Yorkshire my wife called me into the kitchen as she was cooking dinner. From the radio I heard a familiar voice speaking about his life as an Orthodox hermit. It was the monk I had met in Bath. I stood listening to the broadcast realising that I had to get in touch. The next day I made a number of telephone calls and managed to get the number of the hermitage. As we spoke I couldn't be sure if he remembered me from Bath, but he invited me to visit and a date was set.

The track to the hermitage cut through hills and fields and required the driver to repeatedly stop and start to navigate through closed iron gates. Eventually I pulled up besides a newly restored two-storey building and then hesitated before knocking at the door. I was extremely nervous;

around me was complete silence, with no sign of life from within. I knocked and heard hard soles making their way over a wooden floor. The door opened to reveal the tall figure of a monk, his beard past his waist, his thin body dressed in the black robes I had seen in countless photographs. His welcome was warm and genuine, and he closed the door behind me. He generously gave me his whole afternoon, answering my questions and explaining things I didn't even know to ask about. The upper floor of his hermitage was dedicated to the painting of icons, a subject I was quite ignorant about. He explained how each icon expressed not the emotions or sentiments of the individual who painted them, but what the Church believed and what the sacred scriptures express in words. My Protestant thinking found it hard at first to feel comfortable with the veneration of an object in this way, but he helped me to understand that what is being honoured is not the wood and paint, not the material reality in front of us, but the one who is portrayed. The expression "window to heaven" stuck with me; I began to see through the icons into the greater reality that the icons allow us to penetrate. Later I was to discover that early in its history the Church had dealt with the objections raised to icons. He made clear to me that icons are also an expression of our faith in God incarnate. Since Christ came to earth in flesh and blood the very substance of the created order is now drawn up into our offering of worship. Also Christ came with a real face. He was a man in time and space, and so icons are a statement of belief that God has chosen to reveal Himself in a way that can be seen with the physical eyes. He became one of us. My lack of knowledge meant I was constantly searching at a point a long way behind where the Church had reached centuries before. What often passes for debate and enquiry is really a rehash of issues that have long since been settled within the Church. Unless we are familiar with how the Church resolved these questions we can waste our time going over the same old ground.

The hermit patiently responded to everything I asked about. He fed me, gave me a few parting gifts, and with a grateful heart I headed back towards South Yorkshire. In the car I found I couldn't listen to music or even the news on the radio. His presence had been so full of the Holy Spirit that I could only pray. Once again I had tasted the holiness of God in Orthodox people and found myself longing for more of God myself.

Towards the end of my curacy I was coming to the conclusion that I had to act on this growing realisation. I had now read about the many divergences that western Christianity had taken from the authentic faith of the ancient Church, including the insertion of the filioque into the creed. I was now a minister who was unable to say aloud the creed of his church: I stood leading worship unable to declare the faith of the people who had ordained me. Every time I prayed the same issues arose and I found that peace of mind was something I knew infrequently.

And so I was put to the test and failed. My conscience told me that there was only One Church and that I had been granted the grace to find it. But here I was having interviews for the post of vicar in a group of Herefordshire parishes. So much for the clarity of vision I had had about death! I now had two sons and the Church of England paid my wage and provided me with a house. My worldly concerns outweighed my desire to be faithful to God. I no longer even believed that the Church of England was part of the Church. I saw it as a heretical schism from one more schism before that. At my final interview the archdeacon noted that I was from a "Forward In Faith" parish and asked how I would feel working alongside female clergy. I looked him in the eye, and with absolute and complete honesty I said "I believe their ordination is as valid as mine." The panel all nodded approval at my answer, I'm only surprised they could make out what I was saying, speaking with such a forked tongue.

It took me another five years to finally work up the courage to leave. The pull of the world's comforts was stronger than I had imagined, but as I approached the age of forty I knew I had to finally live out what I believed. I had been having discussions with the local bishop about admitting children to communion and he had firmly said no. One morning I was celebrating Holy Communion when a couple of primary school children lifted their hands to receive just as they had seen their parents do a moment before. I felt a powerful urge to give them what they wanted and what I thought they should have, but instead I placed my hand on their heads and blessed them. After the service I felt ashamed. I knew the idea that they had to have a rational understanding of what they were doing was nonsense. Half the congregation that morning would have struggled to give an adequate explanation of what they'd done. The church I belonged to was demanding that I turn children away because they hadn't yet been confirmed. Not long after this I witnessed an Orthodox priest gently spooning communion to a baby and I knew it was right. Orthodox do not separate chrismation from baptism. When a person is received into the Church they receive the Holy Spirit regardless of their mental capacity or age.

The pressure built until I finally sat down and wrote a list of all the reasons why I was still in the Church of England, and those for why I should be Orthodox. While the latter was full of everything I believed, the reasons to stay were about money and fear. I shook my head and the decision was made. When a husband tells his wife that he is giving up his job and pension and that she will lose the house there is never a certainty about how she will react. To her eternal credit my wife agreed that we had to be true to our faith. I was truly blessed.

I then made arrangements to meet with the bishop. I had heard horror stories about how some of them have reacted to this kind of news and was tense. He listened to my reasons for leaving and then tried to persuade me to stay for at least another year so that he could make changes to the group of parishes. It was a terrible temptation, but despite my weakness I managed to refuse. He accepted my decision and then disappeared into his office. He emerged a few moments later clutching a cheque for a thousand pounds "To help us on our way." It was an unexpected gesture and in the coming months when we had to find a house that gift of money kept us afloat. It was one more reason why I am grateful for my time as an Anglican. They gave me a theological education, they nurtured my faith, they housed and fed my family, and I was privileged to be allowed into the most private moments of people's lives. But most of all I am grateful for the many prayerful and devout people I encountered who taught me how to live closer to God. I was not becoming Orthodox because I thought for a moment that I was better than anyone belonging to the church I was leaving behind. I had to become Orthodox because I had not a single doubt that it is the one true faith, the one Church established by the apostles, and that without its guidance and sacraments I knew I was trying to live a Christian life without the help God was offering. In 2002 I resigned from my post and began worshipping in the local Greek Orthodox parish. Of all places, back in Shrewsbury. It was a period of financial difficulty, struggles appeared one after another. But within this testing time God gave us peace of heart, we knew we were home, and no matter what the world did to us we were part of Christ's Church.

Eight years later at my ordination to the priesthood the Archbishop renamed me Spyridon. My father had once told me that my mother had chosen my name Darren Stephen from an American television series *Bewitched* that she had been a fan of during the pregnancy. So I swapped the name of a witch's husband for the name of one of the great heroes of the First Ecumenical Council. As deals go I knew that this had been a good one.

"He who has become the servant of the Lord will fear his Master alone, but he who does not yet fear Him is often afraid of his own shadow."

- Saint John Climacus.

Chapter Four

The desire to visit Mount Athos had been growing over many years. Even though I was now Orthodox it still seemed an unlikely thing to ever happen. I had read and been told about the unwelcoming bureaucracy, about the paperwork that must be picked up in Thessalonica before travelling to Athos, and now that I was ordained I needed a letter of approval for my trip from both my Archbishop and the Ecumenical Patriarch in Constantinople. And because I was now working as a teacher it would mean travelling when the airfares shoot up which made the cost seem impossible.

In November of 2012 a van pulled out in front of me and I was involved in a head-on collision. The insurance payment for my injuries meant the cost was no longer an issue. Once again my understanding wife, despite never having had a single trip abroad as a family, immediately encouraged me to go. I wrote to our Archbishop who took care of arranging things with Constantinople for me. Within a couple of months a timetable was forming and it was time to contact

Greece. I did as much internet research as I could, and collected every detail I could find. Most of the information would turn out to be wrong but having sheets of paper with prices and addresses gave me a certain amount of confidence.

I printed out a map of Athos and studied it carefully. The ferry would take me to a port called Daphne, and as I had romantic ideas about walking between monasteries I chose those that were closest to the port. I knew nothing about them, their reputation or even if they were Greek or Russian. They looked to be within walking distance of each other and that was sufficient criteria for me. I also printed off a list of the telephone numbers of all the monasteries, information freely available on the internet.

Visitors must first ring the Pilgrim's Bureau, which my downloaded material told me was in Thessalonica. I put in the call and on the other side of Europe a man answered in Greek but then switched to perfect English when I announced who I was. He was courteous and business-like and explained that I must first contact the monasteries directly and have confirmation of where I would be staying before he could arrange my permit. I thanked him and then rang the monastery closest to Daphne: Xiropotamou. The telephone rang some time before being answered and I wondered if I was calling at a time when the monks would be in church. But eventually a softly spoken monk answered who took my details and confirmed my stay. It was a good feeling even speaking over so many miles to a monk on Athos, I felt closer to being there already.

There was no response from the second of the monasteries that I tried, but then I managed to make bookings for accommodation at Osiou Grigoriou and then Simonos Petra. This final monastery also faxed me a letter of confirmation that they instructed me to bring along on my trip. I had read about checkpoints leading to certain monasteries where visitors were refused entry without the proper paperwork. It was good to have something official to show that I was legitimate.

Greece is a couple of hours ahead of the UK and it was now too late to ring Thessalonica back. I left it to the following day and happily gave the details of my intended stay. Again the voice on the other end was calm and polite and since I had read that it is a good idea to confirm the booking of permits before leaving home, I asked when it was best to ring back. He dismissed my concerns and suggested I contact them again a couple of weeks before my visit. I felt anxious about this as I would have to buy my air tickets before being certain that I would be allowed on to Athos, but there was nothing more I felt I could do.

In fact I decided to ring back about a month before I was due to travel and to my horror was told that they had no record of me or of my intended visit. It was suggested that I try again in a week when the man's colleague would be back from his holidays. I tried to be patient but it was an anxious few days. Eventually I rang again and the second voice confirmed that there was no record of my visit. I told him I had sent faxes of my passport and letters from the Patriarch. He asked for my email address and said he would be in touch. The Greek approach to life is renowned for being somewhat laid back in comparison with the English attitude, and this taste of its reality was extremely unwelcome.

It was another two days before I received an email assuring me that all was fine and that a permit would be issued for my visit. I printed this off and was determined to have it with me when I arrived at his desk. I made a further call a week before I flew and again was told that there was no record of me. I told the man in Greece of my email and he calmly handed me over to his colleague again. The voice sounded amused at my concerns and promised that all would be well. I began to wonder what would happen if he wasn't at work the day I arrived, and until I had that permit in my hand anxiety never left me.

I selected a couple of suitable books and stuffed them with my other belongings into a nylon duffle bag. I wanted to take as little as possible as I knew I would be carrying it between monasteries. The ticket prices meant it was cheaper to stay in a hotel over night in London rather than fly from an airport closer to home and it was also the only place to get direct flights to Thessalonica. A few rides with British rail and I was at Gatwick Airport. It had taken a whole day to get there and I was glad to have a bed in which to collapse. The flight was at seven a.m. which meant I had to be up about five a.m. in order to book in. I was excited but also apprehensive. Other than the Holy Land I hadn't been abroad since my childhood and here I was setting off alone. I wondered how I would cope with not being able to speak Greek and all the time I kept imagining the man in the Pilgrim's Bureau shaking his head and saying "Sorry, we have no record of your intended visit."

I laid out my typed itinerary on the bed beside me and followed my plans step by step. I had hotel numbers, bus fares; everything that I thought I needed to know was there in black and white. I set my alarm clock and managed to get about four hours sleep before it went off beside me. I jumped to my feet and realised that the next bed I would sleep in would be in Ouranoupolis, a ferry ride from the Hoy Mountain.

As the aeroplane banked left I got my first view of Greece. I was struck by how much empty space there is and how the buildings in the villages and small towns are huddled in small communities each clearly defined and separate from the next. In England we have become used to towns and cities sprawling into one another so that it's sometimes hard to be sure where one ends and another begins. I also hadn't realised just how small the Greek population is compared to that of UK.

We made a bumpy landing and through the small window I could see the intense sunlight illuminating the world. Unlike at UK airports, at

41

Thessalonica there is no mechanical extension to meet the doorway. We descended the steps and then crowded into a waiting bus that carried us to the terminal building. The heat in my face was a reminder that I was no longer near the Atlantic Ocean, until that moment my mind hadn't fully grasped what three hours on an aeroplane really means.

An official took a brief look at my passport and then I was out through the glass doors and into Greece. I wandered over to the line of waiting taxis and the driver was pleased to confirm that he could speak English. I read the name of the bus station and he encouraged me to climb in. I wasn't entirely confident I had requested to be taken to the right station and so asked

"Do the buses go to Ouranoupolis from there?"

"You are going to Mount Athos?" He asked.

"Yes, have you been?"

"Of course," he smiled, "many times. When are you catching the ferry?"

"Tomorrow morning," I said, "will I be able to pick up my permit from the Pilgrim's Office in time?"

"No, no," he shook his head; you must pick up the permit today ready for in the morning." I was alarmed at this news as it was now nearly one o'clock and I had read that the office closed early.

"Will the bus get me there on time?" I asked.

"No, I don't think so. There is not another bus now for two hours, you will miss the office." My heart sank and I felt a slight panic. "I drive people

42

to Ouranoupolis." He announced. "For pilgrims I do a special deal. Normally it would cost one hundred and thirty euro, but I will take you for a hundred and ten. Do you want me to take you?"

I thought for a moment, it was a lot of money, something I hadn't budgeted for. But then I decided the best plan was always to stick to your original plan unless you're certain it isn't going to work.

"No thank you," I said, "that's very kind of you to offer but I will wait for a bus."

He pursed his lips slightly as if to say, "So be it" and in about ten more minutes he pulled off the road into a carpark. Beside the entrance was a small shrine containing an icon but we were passed it so quickly I couldn't make out which saint was being honoured there. The words "bus station" had created an expectation of something slightly grander than the reality revealed itself to be. It was no more than a single grey building surrounded by dusty concrete. I paid the taxi driver and entered the offices through large glass doors. Inside there were about thirty people sheltering from the sunlight. A long counter stretched across one end of the room with three ladies serving customers from behind a plate of thick glass. As I approached I discovered a small icon of Christ stuck to the inside of the window. This gave me enormous confidence, I felt reassured to know that I was in a land where faith could be so openly displayed. I bought a return ticket to Ouranoupolis (which was much cheaper than any of the pilgrim's guides had led me to expect) and was told it would be leaving in fifteen minutes. My suspicions about the taxi driver were confirmed and I felt very content to sit outside beside a few other passengers waiting for the bus. Less than twenty minutes before this I had been on an aeroplane, and here I was already on my way. I started estimating the possible time of arrival in Ouranoupolis and felt sure I would make it before the office closed.

As I sat making my calculations a bearded man in dirty clothing approached me. He held out his hands and asked for my blessing. I made the sign of the cross over him and he kissed my hand before turning and wandering back to where he had been standing. This small event had a profound effect on me. A part of me had been feeling something of an impostor, being English but dressed as an Orthodox priest. But this request for a blessing made me realise none of that nonsense was important: I was ordained to serve people in exactly this way.

An old, rusty bus pulled alongside us and I overheard a Russian man asking where it was headed. At the mention of Ouranoupolis I climbed aboard and folded my rassa beside me. I could see a collection of crosses, prayer ropes and cardboard icons in front of the driver's seat and once again the open display of faith felt reassuring. A few minutes later the bus was half filled, mainly with middle-aged Greek ladies, and we pulled out into traffic while a young conductor wearing jeans and a tee shirt made his way down the bus selling tickets. He flirted with the younger women and seemed to be genuinely enjoying his work. At each

44

small village the bus stopped to pick up more passengers, and each time he made his way down again, smiling and flirting. It was good to see someone so relaxed and comfortable in what they were doing.

The Greek countryside from Thessalonica to Ouranoupolis is made up of arid hills and fields, most of which seem untouched by any attempt at farming. Half-built houses were everywhere, and I wondered if this was a sign that things were looking up for the locals or if the building work had been abandoned as the state of the economy grew worse. One thing I was to discover was that in Greece, it is very easy to strike up a conversation with strangers: just ask what they think of the bankers or the government and they are happy to let you know. The countryside reminded me a little of parts of Israel, or even scenes from spaghetti westerns: the ground is golden and green shrubbery is everywhere. Along the road I lost count of the shrines I spotted. Most were in excellent condition, recently white-washed, with icons and sometimes flowers invoking the prayers of the saints and inviting the prayers of the faithful. I didn't see a single one that was damaged or in any way vandalised which surprised me because on almost all of the uninhabited buildings there was teenagers' graffiti. The secular atmosphere of England suddenly struck me as utterly impoverished as I tried to absorb the reality of a culture and people so comfortable with their Christian heritage. There was no sense of apology or embarrassment, no need for politically sensitive acknowledgement of multi-culturalism, just the open expression of the nation's faith. There are many things I love about English culture, but its self-conscious awkwardness in the way it deals with matters of spirituality isn't one of them.

After nearly two hours of winding our way along the dusty narrow roads the driver announced that we were approaching our final destination. Just then the glittering, blue sea came into view as we came over the rise of a hill and I found myself staring at its beauty.

"Excuse me Father," the voice came from a thin man in the seat behind mine, his thick accent was eastern European. "Are you going to Mount Athos?" He stood and moved to stand alongside my seat.

"Yes," I replied, "and you?"

"Yes Father," he continued, "I have come from a monastery I was visiting in Russia last week. A monk there told me I should visit Mount Athos and so I have come."

"You decided to come last week?" I repeated back to him.

"Yes, he told me I should visit."

I felt anxious for him as I remembered the procedure I had had to go through in order to arrange my permit. "Have you contacted the Pilgrim's Office?"

"No," he shook his head without any sign of concern, "do you think that will be a problem Father?"

"I don't know," was the best I could offer him. "This is my first visit and I'm not sure how things are done." He was perhaps in his late twenties, and the thought of him coming so far only to be turned away was difficult to accept. I wasn't confident for his success, but couldn't bring myself to be the one to break it to him.

As we began chatting the bus pulled into a town square and the doors slid open. There were people sitting outside bars eating meals and couples walking together holding hands. Beside the road a yellow Byzantine fort towered over the whole scene. The immediate sense was of a holiday destination, which I hadn't expected.

A tall blonde man in his early twenties approached us and asked if we knew where to find the Pilgrim's Bureau. He was Russian and spoke very little English. We told him we didn't but agreed to join him in his search. The man from the bus relayed his story once more of how he had come at the suggestion of the monk, and the Russian laughed.

"You have made no arrangements?" He blurted.

"No, I thought I could do that here."

The Russian looked at me and laughed again, "We will have to be careful of this one; I think he is a little crazy." I smiled at the forthright way he was dealing with him.

The three of us headed up a narrow road lined with gift shops and bars. I asked an old man for directions and he came out into the middle of the road to point the way. The Pilgrim's Bureau was now located here in Ouranoupolis which made picking up the diamonitirion (pilgrim's entrance permit) much easier. Eventually we found the office but it was shut. The sign on the door said it was open at eight-thirty in the morning, which would give plenty of time to then catch the ferry. I had read on the internet that this permit had to be confirmed the day before departure for Athos and I could feel a low sense of anxiety fluttering in my stomach. We found the office where ferry tickets would be bought, and feeling secure about where I would be heading in the morning, I decided to find my hotel. It turned out that neither of them had booked places to stay and they were going to simply knock on a few hotel doors and ask if there was any room. I shuddered at the thought of leaving things to the last minute that way, and was slightly relieved to be free of the uncertainty that seemed to surround them as we parted company.

As I walked along the sea front I could see boats moored on the beach beside families in their bathing costumes exposing themselves to the unforgiving sun. A man called out to me from a bar and I politely waved to him. He called out again in Greek but when he discovered I was English he trotted out to catch up with me.

"You are English Father? Have you come to visit Mount Athos?"

I confirmed both assumptions were correct. "You must come and drink some wine with me tonight, that is my bar over there." He pointed to the establishment from which he had just emerged.

"Come tonight and relax before Athos Father." He gave me his card and with great warmth said goodbye. I wondered if he was offering me a drink or just drumming up business for his bar, and in the end assumed the latter.

After wandering up and down a series of very narrow streets it was a great relief to stumble across my hotel. It was a small two-storey building with a line of balconies protruding from the second floor rooms. The reception desk was unattended and I glanced around the many icons on the walls and behind the desk. There were also large colour prints of monasteries framed and for sale, which made my growing excitement at being so close to Athos increased further.

I rang the bell at the desk and a young woman with tightly cropped hair appeared. I gave my name and in a thick Russian accent she informed me that they had no booking for me. I explained that I had made reservations many weeks before, but still she insisted that there was no room for me. Seeing that I wasn't about to just turn and leave she made a telephone call to her boss and asked me to take a seat. She brought out a glass of water and set it before me, for which I was very grateful. A few minutes later a short, stocky man appeared and the two of them began talking about me. He looked through the book in which she had previously tried to find my name and then addressed me for the first time.

"You say you made a booking, who with?"

"I don't know the name of the person I contacted," I explained, "I received emails saying I was booked in."

"Do you have them with you?" He asked.

"The emails? No, I didn't print them off."

It was hard to judge what he was thinking and I wondered if they thought I was pulling a fast one.

"Okay, you sit down, I'll see what I can do." He pointed to the chair in front of the water and rang someone on his mobile 'phone. As I sat there I realised I had left my rassa on the bus. I jumped up and announced what I had done.

"Go quickly," he said, "the bus will still be there. Leave your bag, we will take care of it." My passport and all the money I had brought with me was pushed down inside that bag, and no matter how rude it seemed, I wasn't about to leave it in the hands of strangers. I took out the envelope containing my cash and documents, and ran back to where the bus had dropped us off. When I got there the square was empty and I had seen my rassa for the last time. I arrived back at the hotel red in the face and sweating.

"Come with me," the man said, "there is a room at my father's hotel."

We walked just two minutes down the road to another hotel and he introduced me to a man who looked like an older version of himself. I felt slightly embarrassed at having removed my money before leaving, but this was quickly replaced with a feeling of gratitude and relief. I followed the directions to my room and was pleased with what I found. A double bed, a balcony looking out over the sea, and everything was clean and fresh. I showered and stretched out on the bed, I knew where I had to go in the morning, and everything had fallen into place. I managed to laugh at losing my rassa and decided that if I had to buy another then I was in the right place. The day had exhausted me and checking my alarm clock was two hours ahead of home, I quickly fell to sleep.

"God's desire to save you is incomparably greater than that of your enemy to destroy you."

- Nicodemus of the Holy Mountain.

Chapter Five

The hotel was silent as I made my way down to reception. An older man I hadn't seen before took my key and as I paid him he wished me luck for my journey. Even at eight in the morning the air was warm and the sky as bright as always. A chemist's shop had a large digital thermometer suspended above its door that declared that the day had already reached thirty degrees. Three male bathers passed me in the street as they headed back to their hotel and it struck me as making good sense to enjoy a swim before the sun was at maximum strength. They chatted in Russian as their wet feet patted along the road and they didn't pay me any attention.

I retraced my steps from the previous evening and found the Pilgrim's Bureau already open. It was a long room, a single counter running its entire length where five men were dealing with pilgrim's requests for access to Athos. Along the middle of the room was a long wooden bench that we were meant to sit on while waiting for our turn. But at this time of morning it was empty and I was able to walk directly to the counter. I gave my name and slid my passport to the official. He pushed it back and indicated that I should go to the far end of the counter where a man sat in front of a computer screen. The scene was nothing like I had imagined from my telephone conversations with the staff here when I was back in England, and I still carried the nagging fear that my request for a permit would be refused.

I repeated my name to the second official, he told me the price of the paperwork, and as I handed the euros over he presented me with my documentation. I had read that only one hundred and forty pilgrims are allowed to visit the peninsula each day (only ten of these may be non-Orthodox) and at the time I had considered this a small number. But now, seeing the layout of the bureau, I could imagine quite a chaotic scene when the rush began: it was a scene I was to witness for real in a few days time.

The diamonitrion was an extremely elegant A4 size document of light yellow paper. At its head were three official coloured stamps: a Byzantine two headed eagle, an image of the Theotokos holding Christ and an image of Athos by the sea above which floated angels on clouds. The Greek script was impenetrable to me but I didn't care, it was the assurance of a trip to Athos and holding it lifted every trace of stress from me. Suddenly I felt nothing but relief and calm and there wasn't a piece of paper on earth more valuable to me at that moment. On the back was a list of numbered items that I guessed were rules governing behaviour while on the peninsula. I assumed that I was unlikely to face any situation where I might be breaking them and ignored them.

I took the little side road down to the ferry booking office and discovered I had a forty-minute wait before it opened. I sat down on the wooden step outside the office and looked over my permit one more time. A plump woman in her fifties called to me and pointed to the shaded tables across the road.

"I'm sorry, I don't understand," I repeated yet again.

"Please have a seat Father," she called, "I will bring you a drink."

It struck me as a very civilised idea and I relocated to a bamboo chair overlooking the bay. The woman appeared with a drink's menu and I ordered a lemonade. When it arrived the glass was full of ice and sliced fruit and I happily sat sipping as I watched the waves stroking the sand. From my vantage point I could see the small harbour, more a jetty than a real harbour, and there were a number of men climbing into the cabin of a twenty-foot speedboat. Each day this leaves earlier than the main ferry and I wondered about where the men had started their journeys to be here.

Eventually the ticket office opened and through a small window from a man behind a grill I obtained my little blue ferry ticket. He looked at my permit, took my money and never said a word. I decided to sit on the beach for a while until it was time to leave but as I crossed the road a young man approached me. He began to speak rapidly and held his hand over his chest to let me know some sorrow had befallen him. I explained that I couldn't understand and in English he said, "I have no money."

I thought he was just looking for a handout but before I could reach into my pocket and give him a few euros he told me more. "I have come to visit Mount Athos but I have no money left Father. I need to pay for my diamonitrion."

I had a suspicion I was being taken for a ride, and so rather than hand over whatever he wanted I said "Come on then, let's go and buy your permit." I strode off ahead of him, convinced I was going to call his bluff once we reached the bureau. We joined the small queue that had now formed and then when it was our turn I told him to go ahead and give his details. To my surprise he was greeted with the same instruction to move down to the other end of the counter as I had received earlier and I realised he was genuine. I paid for his permit and walked outside. He caught up with me but instead of thanks he said with expectancy

"I have no money for the ferry."

I almost laughed as I gave him the euros. He bowed slightly and asked for a blessing, and then quickly headed off to purchase his ferry ticket. The actual sum of money that this encounter had cost me was small, but it made me realise how suspicious I could be of strangers.

I bought a pastry and some bottled water from a restaurant, and found a quiet spot on the beach where I could eat my breakfast. A few pilgrims were beginning to gather at the dock as departure time drew closer. Amongst them I saw a small monk carrying a heavy looking rucksack, he stood off to one side and as I discreetly tried to observe him I watched him making the sign of the cross. Even from a distance I could make out the movement of his lips and knew he was reciting the Jesus Prayer.

As I sat watching him a dark shape appeared to my right and I turned to see a large Rottweiler loping over the sand toward me. Only one dog has ever bitten me in my life and it happened to have been an ill-tempered Rottweiler. I froze and tried to decide whether to become fierce in the hope of discouraging his advance or let him have his way with my food – and possibly me. As he came close he started sniffing and I broke a piece off my pastry and threw it slightly passed him so that he had to turn away from me. He twisted back and swallowed the offering without chewing. Immediately it began to move towards me again so I stood up in the hope of at least avoiding a bite to the face. I handed over the remains of my breakfast that he proceeded to eat off the sand. He raised his nose to locate any further food and I held my hands before me, fingers parted to show they were empty. Satisfied he had taken everything I had to offer he bounded off towards the main road. I walked quickly over to the steps back up to the harbour and hoped that by mingling with other people the dog would be less likely to find me.

The ferry was already at the dock but I hadn't realised it was our boat; it looked to me like a cargo freighter rather than something to carry human beings. Its name was the Axion Esti, which I knew means "worth it is", a hymn sung at Divine Liturgy. What I didn't know was that it is also the name of a renowned icon at the cathedral of Karyes, the capitol of Athos. I made my way over and joined the crowd that was preparing to board. One of the crew stepped off onto the quay and immediately signalled that I should come aboard. I showed my ferry ticket and he asked to see my permit. Satisfied with this he waved me on and I strolled ahead towards the back of the ferry in the hope of shade. As I climbed the iron steps to the upper decks I looked back and realised that no one else had yet been permitted to board and once again I sensed the legitimacy of my priesthood in this place. I made my way to the upper deck and leaned on the white iron railing to watch the other pilgrims being allowed aboard. Amongst them I spotted the blonde Russian man from the night before but he was alone. I felt sad for the other man who I imagined was now sitting in his hotel room wondering where to go next.

The pilgrims reached the bottom of the steps that led up to the floor I was on and since I estimated there were only about forty seats available I chose one in the shade and made myself comfortable. The seats around me were quickly filled and then we sat for about twenty minutes before the deep rumble of the engines came to life. At nine forty-five the ferry backed slowly away from the land, and made a slow arc as it headed out across the water to Athos.

"Cleave to the saints, for they who cleave to them shall be made holy."

- Saint Clement of Rome.

Chapter Six

Stepping off the ferry on to the dusty ground of Athos was not a moment I was able to romanticise or pause to reflect on. The crowd of pilgrims was quickly making its way towards three buses parked about fifty metres from the shore. I was caught up in the flow of bodies until we reached the broad space in front of a group of three shops. To my right stood a building used as a customs office outside of which two men in uniform stood chatting, showing no interest of any kind in the new arrivals. Outside one of the shops were tables and benches where around half a dozen men sat drinking in the shade of the building.

The Russian priest from the ferry appeared at my side and asked

"Which monastery are you visiting first?"

"Xiropotamou," I replied, confidently pointing back along the coastline that the ferry had just been following.

"Then you must take one of those buses," he instructed me.

"No," I smiled, "I'm going to walk between monasteries."

He shook his head with a look of such concern that my sense of objection was overcome. "Quickly," he continued, "get on the bus before it is full. It is too hot and too far to walk." The image of the map that I had printed back at home sprung to my mind and I remembered that it hadn't seemed so far. But I trusted his advice and trotted over to the nearest bus.

"Are you going to Xiropotamou?" I called up to the driver, feeling very self-conscious about my pronunciation in front of the seated pilgrims.

"Yes," he nodded.

I climbed the steps and found the seat behind the driver was empty. Beside me sat another, older Russian priest who stared ahead without wanting to engage with anyone. A man who had been loading bags into the side of the bus then appeared at the doorway and began selling tickets to the seated passengers. The price was exactly the same as I had paid to ride the ferry all the way from Ouranopolis and I decided I would stick to walking from now on. The driver waited until his colleague had returned to the front before starting up the big diesel engine that grumbled into life. The interior was stifling but the driver left the door open, and once we had started to move a cool draught began make its way in amongst us.

The road climbed steeply and as we passed small groups of pilgrims I began to be grateful for my seat and for the insistence of my Russian friend. The view out over the sea was spectacular but as I kept looking ahead for glimpses of the monastery I could see nothing. I imagined the distance must be much greater than I had imagined but after only ten minutes' driving we pulled over and the conductor called out the name of Xiropotamou.

Two other men climbed down behind me, we stepped back to avoid the cloud of dust coming from the wheels and watched as the bus lurched off to the next monastery. We nodded our acknowledgement of each other and then I headed back to look out over Daphne that now seemed a long way down beneath us. I watched as the ferry was reversing out into the water, making its wide turn before heading back to Ouranoupolis. I could see the passengers sitting aboard and it brought home to me how short my stay here was to be. I was determined to make the most of my visit, but I wasn't sure exactly what that would entail or what to expect. The questions I had imagined had brought me here were gone, and I was left to simply experience and learn all that I could without any presuppositions.

The oddest realisation that I had at that moment was that no matter how spectacular the scenery, no matter how beautiful the sea, this really was just another place. A strangely obvious thing to think, but I had been so full of expectation I must have anticipated an immediate impression of something special. But I didn't and it wasn't. It was a piece of land with air and dust just like any other dusty road. And as lacking in profundity as that may seem it hit home to me that the men who commit their lives to monasticism here are in no way escaping reality. My skin, my eyes, everything that I had arrived from England with was exactly the same here as it had been at home: and the struggles with temptation and sin were also something I had carried with me. Athos is not a place where men go to escape themselves, it is where they meet and confront themselves in all their reality and truth. The sense of this struck me hard and the magnitude of the monastic task assumed a greater depth. It also made me realise how much of a fantasy my expectations had created, as though simply to walk on this holy ground would fill me with mystical experiences. In fact the reality of its ordinariness was far more important because it connected everything here with normal life and the world full of people struggling to make sense of their lives.

The other two pilgrims had by this time disappeared, being far too sensible to hang around in the sun like this daft Englishman. There was a broad path heading round a bend and I assumed that this must be the road to take. As I came round the corner I saw the first building but there was still no sight of the monastery itself. From beside the single-story structure a locked gate extended across the road and an arrow pointed to the right with instructions in Greek script. I assumed it was pointing the way and climbed a few concrete steps to a roofed porch. There was a low wooden bench and I was about to set up my camera and take a picture of myself with the woods behind me when I caught sight of a security camera looking down at me from the corner of the ceiling. I felt embarrassed to have been messing around trying to take a picture and made my way out and along the narrow path that another sign and arrow seemed to be indicating was the way to go. Someone had once told me that visitors to Athos fall either into the category of pilgrim or tourist and I knew at that moment I had been behaving like the latter.

On either side of the path the ground rose in high yellow banks making it impossible to guess where the route was headed. But turning the final corner the whole monastery suddenly came into view only thirty or so metres away. A large stone-floored area led to an impressive and ancient looking building. The ground floor wall was windowless and resembled a medieval castle, fortified and impenetrable. On top of this sat a broader floor that extended out like a balcony or the captain's cabin on an old sailing ship. This upper floor was painted blue and pink, colours that looked playful against the sombre looking stone. There wasn't a soul to be seen so I headed towards a gate in the wall that ran along the edge of the yard. On the other side I found a dark, wooden doorway every bit as medieval-looking as the stone walls.

At the door hung another sign in Greek and it seemed only logical that it must be for visitors rather than permanent inhabitants, and as there was no bell or knocker, I let myself in. It took my eyes a moment to adjust to the sudden darkness inside, and I found myself next to a small wooden office with frosted glass that looked like the reception areas found the world over. There was an electronic button, the kind that operates doorbells, and so I pressed it. A couple of minutes later a young monk, perhaps in his early thirties, appeared from another door and made his way down to where I was standing. His face was sculpted by a life of serious fasting, and I knew I was in the presence of someone whose life was lived with a level of commitment lacking in my own.

He spoke very gently in Greek, and I began my pattern of explanation about being English. He switched languages.

"You are a priest?"

"Yes, I have a letter from the Ecumenical Patriarch."

He took the paper from me, "Have you made a reservation for tonight?"

"Yes," I said, "I rang a couple of months ago."

"One moment please," he entered the little wooden office and quietly closed the door behind him. A minute or so later he reappeared, "Please follow me."

He led me along the dark corridor and out to a white walled room where another pilgrim was sitting.

"Please sit here," said the monk, "I will bring you some refreshments."

As I sat the other visitor avoided eye contact and I noticed an empty tray in front of him. The room was immaculately clean, with large windows in the wall behind us allowing light to fill the air. A short while later the monk returned carrying a metallic tray. He placed a small table directly in front of me and placed my refreshments there. I thanked him and then he asked the other pilgrim to go with him. On the tray were a large glass of cold water and a plate containing five pieces of loukoumi; in England we call this Turkish Delight. Each piece was crusted in white coconut and was absolutely delicious. Had I been sharing the treat with another person I would never have dared to have taken so much and it gave a powerful impression of generosity. The only gift my wife had asked me to bring her back from Greece was Turkish Delight, and as I sat eating so much of it in my first Athonite monastery I smiled at the thought of her.

The water cut through my thirst and I sat quietly for about five minutes sensing and trying to engage with the silence around me. The young monk returned and asked me to follow him. We entered a long corridor that had a dark tiled floor, one wall had huge paintings of the monastery hanging on whitewashed plaster, and the other was a series of large wooden windows that looked across at the church. The design of the monastery followed the standard pattern of buildings creating an enclosure in the middle of which sits the church. This one had pink walls and a contrasting light blue roof. It looked pretty but humble, and I found myself twisting my neck to look up at the domed roof that rose up into a cloudless sky.

The monk led me up two flights of stone stairs to a corridor of guest rooms, The walls were a series of light and grey stone and each doorway consisted of an arch in coloured bricks. The attention to detail was impressive, nothing had been left as simply functional or plain, everything carried a small expression of design or architectural flourish. I remembered the grey monotony of high-rise flats in Sheffield and knew that the beauty I was seeing here was more than decoration: it expressed the human need to live in an environment that communicated the worth of the people inhabiting it.

The monk opened one of the doors and gestured for me to enter. As I did so he immediately left and I pulled the door shut behind me. There were three single beds, each with exactly the same towels and sheets folded and placed in precisely the same way as the next. Beside each bed was a pair of slippers that created a sense of homeliness. The one window in the room was small and arched and was positioned in a corner at the head of the bed I chose to sleep in. There was a dark wooden cupboard against the one wall on which sat a large metallic jug and a drinking glass. It was empty and I decided to make sure I had a good supply available so I went off in search of a tap. At the bottom of the stairwell was an old drinking fountain from which I took a drink and then filled the jug. Next to the fountain was a timetable, again in Greek only. I could at least make out the times and saw that something was due to start in thirty-five minutes.

Back in my room I checked out the view from the window and found I could see a skete sitting amongst the trees on the hill above the monastery. I watched it for a while but could detect no signs of life. I made a visit to the toilets on my floor where I washed the day's heat from my face and then returned to lie across the bed and gather my thoughts.

Five minutes before whatever was scheduled was going to start I gathered myself and made my way back to where I had been treated with the loukoumi. There were five other pilgrims sitting along the bench and I smiled and joined them. They quietly chatted amongst themselves in Greek.

"Do any of you speak English?" I asked hopefully.

"Yes, I do," the youngest of the group replied.

"I couldn't read the sign, what is happening first?"

"We will be taken into the church to venerate the icons," he explained, "and then they will feed us."

As he was speaking a white-bearded monk appeared and waved for us to follow him. We crossed to the outer doors of the church and he stood holding them open for us. As we entered we saw that the walls and ceilings were covered in paintings depicting scenes from the Bible as well from various saints' lives. We weren't given time to look at them as the monk led us through another door and I realised that we hadn't even yet entered the church.

The church, and every church that I entered on Athos, consisted of a number of different rooms, each divided from the previous one by a wall that looked like an iconostasis. As you walked through the space that resembled the Royal Doors you drew closer to the actual iconostasis at the eastern end of the building. The sense of drawing closer by degree to a holy space was extremely vivid, and was intensified by the brilliance of the golden icons sitting on the actual iconostasis.

As we entered we found a monk standing behind a low table in front of the Royal Doors. He stared down at the ground, and once we had gathered in front of him he began to speak in Greek. At no point did he look up at us and it was clear that he was running through a script that he performed every day for visitors. Across the table were a large number of different shaped boxes, each containing a holy relic, some of which were surprisingly large. I was used to seeing tiny fragments but some of these looked to be entire bones.

As he came to the end of his speech he invited us to move forward. I was standing at the back of the group and the monk who had led us over to the church touched my arm and told me to go first. Hearing the instruction being given to me in English the monk behind the table asked if I had understood the Greek. I explained that I hadn't and so in an American accent that was quite unexpected he began explaining which saints the relics were from as he moved along the table pointing to each in turn.

"This is a piece of the True Cross," he began, "this is from Saint Polycarp; this is from Saint John Chrysostum; this from Saint Basil the Great, this is the head of Saint Photini, the woman Jesus met at the well, this is from Saint Gregory of Armenia," and there were many others.

I stepped forward and began to perform my metanias (bows involving a reaching to the ground and a turning of the hand) and kissed each relic in turn. The skull of Saint Photini (the Samaritan woman Jesus met at the well) was set into a beautiful case but even that hardly seemed worthy of such an object. The early Church recognised that our salvation is not a reality for the soul or spirit alone, but the whole person including the body. When a saint enters heaven they continue to be connected to their earthly remains in some mysterious way that makes it possible for the Church to draw close to them through their relics.

As I moved my way down the table the other pilgrims followed under the careful watch of the monk. When we had finished he said something in Greek and the others began fishing around in their pockets. I thought they were being asked to make a financial contribution until I saw them pulling out their prayer ropes. They handed them to the monk who started taking each in turn and blessing them on each of the relics. I quickly took out mine and added it to the little pile and watched with joy as my little rope gently caressed these physical contacts with eternity. I took it back from him as a new treasure.

The white haired monk then ushered us out from the church but instead of returning to the waiting room we were taken into a small refectory where a table of food was waiting. The monk indicated that we should serve ourselves and so we filled our plates from the buffet. There were lots of fresh vegetables and fruit, heavy dark bread that smelt like it had just been baked and a bowl of what resembled pancake rolls. I gratefully carried my meal to one of the tables where a few of the other men were sitting. They had already started eating so I crossed myself and blessed the food. It surprised me that there was no communal prayer said and I wondered if I should take the lead. But as they had already started eating I didn't want to make them feel uncomfortable. The white-bearded monk remained behind the table of food, watching to see if he could be of service, but none of the other monks appeared. This was unexpected as I had read accounts of people sharing their meal times with the monks as prayers or spiritual texts were read aloud. A few hushed conversations were shared but most of us ate in silence. The food was delicious. I realise that this is an un-Athonite thing to say. For the monks food is a means to sustaining the body, they eat quickly to avoid becoming too attached to the pleasures of the flesh, but being so deeply immersed in such pleasures I savoured every mouthful.

As I was eating one of the pilgrims stopped beside my table and asked

"Are you English Father?"

"Yes," I replied looking up at him.

He sat opposite me and smiled. "Did you arrive today?"

"Yes, this is my first monastery."

"And is this your first visit to Athos?"

"It is," I confirmed, "what about you, have you been before?"

"Oh yes, I come as often as I can, at least once a year. In Greece it is normal for all men to have visited Athos at least once; it is something we just do."

"You're lucky to have it on your doorstep," I observed, "we don't have anything like this in England."

"Not just England," he said, "there is nowhere else like it anywhere in the world."

I nodded in agreement. "How long have you been here this time?" I enquired.

"For three days, we are going home tomorrow." He pointed to one of the men at the other table where he had been eating, "That is my father, we always come together."

I envied him belonging to a culture where such things could be shared so naturally.

"Which other monasteries have you been to?"

"We have spent our days at the Skete of Saint Anne. My father knows one of the monks and was able to arrange things. It was good to stay in such an intimate setting, it meant we had lots of access to the fathers and they were happy to talk to us. There were two monks we got to know very well. You will find things a little different here." He glanced up at the monk as he said this, perhaps unconsciously checking to see if his comment had been overheard. Perhaps becoming aware of the critical nature of what he had said he added "Xeropotamou is believed to have been founded by

Emperor Pulcheria in 455AD, so it has a long and honourable tradition."

I was impressed with his knowledge and asked "Where does the name Xeropotamou come from?"

"That is from Saint Paul Xeropolamos, a famous hermit here on the Holy Mountain, He approached the Emperor of his day, in the mid-nine hundreds, and persuaded him to build a monastery on this site. Have you heard of Saint Athenasius?" I admitted that I hadn't and he continued to explain.

"He spread the idea of large monasteries on Athos, before him the monks lived alone as hermits. To encourage monasticism he encouraged the building of the kind of monasteries you will see on Athos today. There were many who opposed such a move because they believed it would distract from the original desert ideals of Egypt, but he had the backing of the emperor and thankfully the life of the hermit continues also today."

He noticed his father preparing to leave and so stood himself saying "It is good to have met you, I hope you receive many blessings while you are here. Special things occur here, you will see." I thanked him for everything he had shared with me and he joined his father and another man and the three of them left.

The plates were simply left on the table for the monk to collect and so standing and blessing myself once more I too made my way back to my room. The timetable informed that there was a service at seven o'clock and I decided to take a rest and try and absorb everything that had happened so far. As I lay on the bed I thought about what he had said at the table and recognised a strong sense of expectation in myself. I wasn't sure what to expect, but I knew I hadn't come to Athos only to enjoy the views.

At about half six I washed and generally tried to prepare myself for the first service. The structure of time on the Holy Mountain follows the Byzantine pattern of dividing the day between sunrise and sunset, so that sunset is equivalent to midnight. This means that time here is always between three and six hours ahead of the rest of Greece. As I walked towards the church I understood that Athos is separated from the world even in the passing of time.

I was early for what turned out to be vespers and the church door was locked. It gave me time to look more carefully at the frescoes I had admired earlier. There were images of martyrs being abused in all kinds of ways, demons prodding at saints in prayer, and angels everywhere. The constant theme was the nearness of heaven and earth. As each human struggle ran its course the paintings depicted the reality of heaven watching, rewarding and intervening. It created the strong impression of how all we do in this life is really part of the one cosmic reality stretching beyond life and death, that while we concern ourselves with the world we can see we also live as part of the world that we cannot see. The effect of all this was very positive, even standing there alone, waiting for the church door to be unlocked, I knew I was really standing before

Christ and His angels even as those portrayed in the frescoes were doing. For the men whose lives are dedicated to monasticism, the illusion of separation between those two parts of creation must simply dissolve. Everything they do is focussed on bringing together the two parts of that one reality, heaven and earth.

A monk appeared behind me and nodded reverently to me in a gesture that was filled with dignity and simplicity. I bowed in response and followed him into the church. There was still about fifteen minutes before vespers began and outside I heard the first beating of the symantron. When Ottoman invaders denied Christians the freedom to ring church bells the custom developed of beating a wooden board with a mallet. This tradition continues on Athos. The monk beating the symantron was walking around the outside of the church, creating rhythms that were intricate and beautiful. He turned the wooden board into a musical call to prayer, and in the silence of Athos its voice penetrated every hall and room of every building.

I venerated the icons that shimmered in the light of flickering candles and found myself a place to sit in the middle chamber of the church. Around the walls were wooden stalls with arm rests and seats that folded down to allow the user to either stand and lean against them or fully sit. Soon the black clad monks began to glide gracefully through the church. They looked neither left nor right but bowed to and kissed the icons before disappearing into the next room of the church. A few of the pilgrims joined me in the stalls which lifted any doubts from me that I was standing in the wrong place. I closed my eyes and began to run the knots of my prayer rope through my fingers and so didn't see the monk approaching me. I felt his hand gently grip my arm,

"Father," he whispered, "please come to the front."

I followed him to the stalls in front of the golden iconostasis where the monks were standing. He stopped and asked

"Do you have a rassa Father?"

"No," I said, "I lost mine on the bus coming here."

"We will lend you one for the duration of your stay here." He turned and disappeared to the back of the church.

The monks were positioned on either side of the church, some were bent over in prayer, others glanced around to take a look at the day's visitors. The black shawls were a reminder that they had died to the world, that they were buried now and were waiting for resurrection with Christ. There were no more than twenty of them in total and they were mainly middle-aged or older. Their long white beards gave them an appearance of belonging to another age, and their faces shone with an inner light. I had to force myself to look away as I could happily have sat staring at them for hours. To be in the presence of genuinely holy people is a wonderful blessing; it fills the heart with a longing to be better oneself.

They began to sing, the two groups calling their verses and responses in turn, all in Greek of course. Thankfully many of the prayers included familiar phrases and I was able to follow a tiny proportion of what was happening. But it didn't matter to me that I couldn't understand every word. The prayer went beyond language like the time I had worshipped with the Russians in Bath. The mood and atmosphere was sufficiently affecting that even if a person had never heard of Christianity, the experience of this service would have convinced them that God was present and being worshipped.

The monk reappeared and handed me a rassa to go over my cassock. I slipped it on and caught one of the older monks smiling at me: I realised how foolish I must have looked but I also knew that there was no malice in his smile. I smiled too.

Towards the end of the service the priest moved forward and began to venerate the icons. A monk walked over to me and waved for me to do the same. It was a moment of extreme embarrassment. Not because I didn't know what I was doing, but because it seemed ridiculous that I should be venerating the icons before the other monks. I did as I was asked and a line of monks formed behind me. A wave of joy flooded through me, it was an astonishing feeling to be venerating the Theotokos beside these men. I felt utterly at home, utterly accepted, it was a place I felt I belonged. This was an odd thing to be feeling so soon after being uncomfortable, and I returned to my stall questioning what was happening within me. The other pilgrims filed in and kissed the icons and then the monks began to leave. I followed them out and realised that they were heading off to their cells. I hesitated slightly, not sure of where I should go, but then decided to head back to my own room.

Once there I reflected on what had happened in church and it became clear to me that despite being an ordained priest I still carried the nagging doubt that someone would call me an impostor. I was an Englishman with barely any grasp of Greek. I had been raised without any grounding in authentic Christianity. How could it be possible that the Church could entrust me with such a treasure as the priesthood? And on top of all this I knew only too well what a sinner I was.

But here at the centre of Christian spirituality, here where there was an unquestioned authority recognised the whole world over, my priesthood was a fact. My own personal qualities or background were irrelevant. Priesthood is in no way dependent on some kind of worthiness that the individual might claim. On the contrary, I was a priest simply because Christ's Church had ordained me. The priesthood itself is the possession of Christ, it is the living out of a sublime blessing, and every act of honour that was paid to me was made to the office of the priesthood, not to me personally as a man. I could have repeated these sentiments before coming to Athos, and genuinely have known them to be true, but now they were something I actually understood. It gave me great peace to grasp this and I decided that if I left Athos with nothing else, it had been worth the trip for this alone.

" She is the door of life because Christ the life entered into the world through her."

- Elder Cleopas.

Chapter Seven

I sat looking out of the little window wondering about the men up in the skete. A few insects twitched against the net that was keeping them out but other than the sound of their wings there was the deep silence that I was slowly becoming accustomed to. I set my alarm for three-thirty and pulled a single sheet over myself. It was too warm for anything more even lying under an open window and I quickly fell into a deep and satisfied sleep.

When it rang the alarm was monstrously loud and I jumped to shut it off. Once again the same silence ran along the corridors, across the hills and to the very edges of my senses. I was washed and dressed before the beating of the symantron began, and as they did the rhythms mysteriously called out from the darkness. I stood at one of the windows at a balcony for a moment and watched the monks move like shadows through the dark morning air into the waiting stillness of the church. Tiredness had not yet had a chance to register as I too found my place in the stalls in church. I watched as the last of the monks venerated the icons and settled myself for the hours of prayer.

The singing was deep and resonant, the monks had strong assured voices and the offices began to flow in a stream of Greek words calling out to God. The prayers were punctuated with points where all the monks stepped forwards away from the stalls to prostrate themselves completely. Though I didn't know the prayers, I understood the action and joined them each time as they bent and touched the ground with their foreheads.

The first services lasted about three hours. I had no sense of time, my growing sleepiness and unfamiliarity with the structure of the office meant I was in a kind of timelessness where there was nothing more to do but pray, and nowhere else to be but standing before the icons. Around six in the morning the Divine Liturgy began and the words brought me back to a pattern that was familiar. As each movement of book and incense followed one after another I felt more at home and was able to pray along with the specific details of what was going on. The lighting and extinguishing of different candles was a complicated set of rituals I had never seen before, and from the heights of the ceiling oil lamps were lowered and raised to punctuate the prayers.

Eventually the Royal Doors opened and the priest who had shown us the relics the evening before now stepped out holding the holy cup. I had made no arrangement to receive communion and had heard stories of English priests being turned away from the chalice, so I made no move to join the four monks lining up to receive. Besides, I knew priests must receive communion at the altar, and now it was too late. But I was content to stand in the shadows, unobserved and simply present.

When the Liturgy was nearing its end the priest took his seat on a large wooden throne near the centre of the church and the monks began to move towards him. One monk approached me and again I was invited to join the head of the line. The monk in front of me bowed and kissed the hand of the priest and so I knew what was expected. At my turn I stepped up to him intending to do the same and was surprised when he bent and kissed my hand too. That a holy monk from Athos should kiss my hand as a priest was perhaps the most humbling experience of my life and I still find it deeply moving to think about.

There was a hint of the morning sunlight through the windows high above us near the ceiling. It was after seven and the long night office was over. The other pilgrims were receiving their blessing from the priest who remained bent over throughout, humbly avoiding looking up at the men before him. We made our way back to the refectory and there a layman was now standing behind the table that was again laden with a variety of food. We each carried our filled plates to the tables, and without the watchful gaze of the guest master conversations were enjoyed at normal volumes. The man who had spoken to me the day before sat opposite me to eat and we chatted once again. He explained that he worked for the Greek embassy and again impressed me with his knowledge of Athos. He invited me to join him for coffee but I explained that I intended to walk to the monastery of Osiou Grigoriou that morning and wanted to cover as many miles as possible before the day was too hot. He looked concerned, and told me to be careful.

"Our group climbed to the summit of Mount Athos three days ago," he said, "but I couldn't make it." I was surprised as he looked to be in his early thirties and perfectly healthy. He must have sensed my reaction because he continued "It wasn't the climb or the distance, it was the heat. I am Greek but it was too much for me. Please be careful."

I was touched by his concern and explained my plan of sticking to monasteries within walking distance of each other but he wasn't convinced.

"There is a ferry that leaves quite regularly from Daphne," he informed me, "see how you feel."

"I will, thank you." I rose from the table and we shook hands, I wondered if the formal gesture had seemed alien to him, or if he had assumed this was the way to deal with an Englishman. I collected my duffle bag from the room and then decided to seek out the guest master to ask where I cold leave a contribution in thanks for the monastery's hospitality. He was nowhere to be seen and I considered going back to my room and leaving it next to the bed. Just then a middle aged monk appeared to remind me to return the rassa which I was now carrying over my arm. Knowing that I would be expected to have one at the other monasteries I was visiting I asked if there was any chance of it being for sale but with an extremely serious expression he told me no. I left him with my donation and expressed my gratitude for the visit.

With that I headed back towards the road.

"Father!" the same monk was now shouting me. "You can take a short cut to Daphne if you take that path." He pointed to an area of bushes where no path was visible. I again thanked him and walked over to where he had directed me. There was still no sign of a path but I kept going in the belief that that he must know what he was talking about. Eventually I reached a steep cliff that looked down on a ravine of jagged grey rocks. It was impossible to go any further and I retraced my steps. Once in sight of the monastery I headed back along my original route and out onto the main road. At least I knew where this was headed, and since it was all downhill to Daphne I set off with a feeling of confidence.

As I walked I began to think about the experiences I had just had. I was a little disappointed to have found the monks so distant: I hadn't managed to have a single real conversation with any one of them. Perhaps all that I had read about and hoped for was no more than a fantasy. But spending the night in prayer with the monks had been very special, and I decided in all honesty that if this was to be the nature of my pilgrimage then it was enough. I was genuinely content to settle for this and as I let gravity assist me back towards Daphne I felt a wave of gratitude to God for being permitted to glimpse something of the monks' way of life.

Daphne still looked a long way off and I began to find it hard to imagine how the bus had covered so much distance in so little time. After about forty minutes of walking the sun was beginning to burn stronger and I finished the last contents of my water bottle. Turning the next corner I could see two pilgrims struggling up the road towards me, each carrying a backpack that looked too cumbersome for such a venture. As we approached each other one of them shouted hi and I called hello to them. When we were about to pass each other we stopped and I could hear their panting.

"Where are you going?" I asked.

"To Xiropotamou," the one replied, "is it far?"

"You've got quite a walk ahead of you," I warned them, "where have you come from?"

"We are Italian," the same man replied.

"You are Orthodox?" I asked.

"No Father," and he didn't add anything more to that, perhaps having been warned about uttering the words "Roman Catholic" on the peninsula.

We wished each other well and set off on our separate paths. I wondered about how much more difficult it must have been to have arranged their visit than it had been for me and hoped they found all that they had come for.

I had been descending for just over an hour when I found myself walking past two of the old buses parked at Daphne. I strode towards the café, relieved to see it open. The newly arrived pilgrims who must have caught the early speedboat sat enjoying their drinks. At their feet were half a dozen scrawny looking cats, some lying lazily in the shade, others looking expectantly up at the tables. I knelt down and took a photograph for my wife, something she had made me promise to do if I should encounter Athos moggies.

The café's interior was dark and cool, and behind the counter were countless varieties of cans and bottles of every kind of drinkable fluid. I bought a bottle of water but had swallowed its contents before I had made it to the door. I turned and asked for two more. The man serving smiled, "Hot today?" he asked. I grinned and nodded, grateful for his refrigerator and extremely low prices.

From the restaurant I wandered into the shop next door. It had limited space and I was nervous about catching one of the shelves with my bag. I dumped it next to the till and strolled along the narrow isles. They stocked icons, prayer ropes, incense; everything a pilgrim could want to take back into the world. At the very back of the shop was a glass cabinet that contained a rail of black rassas. I slid my arm around the glass door to feel the material and see if there was a price tag at the collar. As I was doing this a tall, thin man in his twenties appeared at my side.

"Do you want to try one on Father?" I was embarrassed to have my arm in the cabinet, and said "How much are they?"

"Let me see," he said, sliding the glass front open. He pulled one off the rail and announced "One hundred and forty euros." It was a lot more than I wanted to spend but I didn't want to face turning up at another monastery half dressed. He could see my indecision and encouraged me to try it on. It was about two inches too long and the sleeves hung past my knees. He began folding the material on my arms and assured me that with a few pins it would be fine.

"Do you have another size?" I asked.

"No Father, they are all the same."

I slipped out of it and handed it back to him. "I think I'll leave it until I come back."

"But Father, you can't go to the monastery without a rassa. They will think you are just a poor priest who can't afford one."

I smiled at his attempt at persuasion, being considered poor was the least of my worries. I felt the material, it was good quality. Despite my wanting not to be manipulated by his attempt at a sales pitch, I knew I needed it.

"Okay," I nodded, "I'll take it."

The young man looked elated, and I guessed that he was working on commission. "I will wrap it for you Father." He headed back to the till and I continued looking at the rest of his stock. I decided it would be best not to load my bag unnecessarily and walked over to pay.

"What is your name Father?"

"Spyridon," I replied.

"Ah, wait one moment please." He finished carefully wrapping the rassa and handed it to me. It fit comfortably in my bag and having bought it I felt I'd made the right decision. As I stood up from my packing he reached out to offer me something.

"For you, Father, for your journey." It was a small printed icon of Saint Spyridon in his familiar shepherd's hat. I gratefully took it and slipped it into my cassock pocket.

"I will see you again in a couple of days," I promised, "I will buy my family presents before I leave."

"Very good Father, may Saint Spyridon and the Holy Mother be with you. What time is your boat?"

"Do you mean today?" I asked.

"Yes, which boat are you catching?"

"No, I'm walking to Saint Grigoriou." I felt a little proud announcing this.

His face tightened, "No Father, you must not walk, it is too far and too hot."

"How many hours walk is it?" I was less willing to be persuaded by him than I had by the Russian priest.

"About two hours Father, but the ferry will take you round the coast."

"No, I want to walk. Two hours isn't so bad."

He was still shaking his head as I left the shop, I adjusted the strap of my bag so that it went across my chest, and set off along the path to my next monastery. Immediately behind the shops was a small car park where two monks were sitting in a motionless van. They nodded as I passed and then I was hitting the gentle incline towards the rising mountain before me. The gradient increased and within five minutes I was climbing. I bent forward and watched my feet plodding over the yellow dust. After about thirty minutes I realised that I had miscalculated the rate of the sun's climb and it felt pretty much as hot as it cold possibly get. I took regular swigs from one of the bottles of water. Back home I walk in the Welsh hills fairly regularly and knew I could cope with the physical demand of the climb. But the heat was making a much greater demand on me than I had imagined possible.

I started making calculations in my head so that I wouldn't drink my supply too quickly. I judged half a bottle for each half hour of walking and happily gulped away with this in mind. Every so often there were benches fixed into the hillside and I made good use of them. As I came to one corner I was able to look back at the orange roofs of Daphne and beyond the port see the monastery of Xeropotamou nestling in the walnut trees of the hillside. I tried to judge the distance I had covered but it didn't seem to match the amount of time I had been walking.

To accommodate the steep mountainside the road snakes back and forth so that the old monastery vans and buses can negotiate the climb. This means that the walker is forced to double-back on himself repeatedly. I slumped across a wooden bench and checked my water against the time. I had been climbing for an hour and a half and was down to my last portion of water. The road could still be seen winding back and forth up ahead and there was no sign of where it might start to head down to the monastery next to the sea. I could feel my face burning in the sun and decided to remove my cassock. This helped cool me a little, but I was beginning to wonder if I should have taken the shopkeeper's advice.

After another twenty minutes I came across what looked like a short cut that ran directly up rather than twisting left and right like the main road. As long as I kept going forwards I was bound to meet the road again so I headed off up this new path. The surface was now very rocky and uneven and when I checked the time I realised that it had been well over two hours since I had set off. I decided it couldn't be too far now and pushed my self on. There were no longer any benches inviting pilgrims to rest and every ten minutes I allowed myself to sit in the shade where the dirt bank offered protection from the sun.

My clothes were entirely drenched through with sweat and this was causing the material of my trousers to rub against my legs. They felt quite raw and it was beginning to make walking difficult. The time between rests began to shorten and once the water was gone I knew I might be in difficulty. I began to wonder if I was going to make it off the mountain and I laughed to think that having finally made it to Athos I might end up collapsing here. A moment of real panic then struck me as I realised that having left the main road it might be a long time before anyone came this way and found me. I was now only managing around twenty steps between rests and as my pace slowed I knew it meant more time in the sun. My bag was now cutting into my shoulders and I considered dumping anything that was unnecessary for getting back to England.

I lay in the shade of a rock amongst strange flowers that I couldn't identify, everything seemed alien. Realising now the true gravity of the situation I began to pray. I felt calm but at risk and knew I didn't want to be found dead. I prayed to the Theotokos and felt her presence. She was near in a way I had never known before; I could sense her presence as I had only ever previously sensed the presence of God. It was an enormous comfort and all fear or panic left me. I continued to struggle, a few paces at a time, praying constantly now. My body had nothing left to offer, it was only by the power of my will and the comfort of the Mother of God that I was able to continue.

I kept making it to ridges that I was convinced would be the final climb only to discover another one half a mile ahead of me. Eventually I could see the road again and was glad to be back on the official route. Dehydration and sun stroke combined to make me dizzy and I found I was staggering a little. In this pathetic condition I rounded a corner and found the Monastery of Simonos Petra sitting far ahead of me like a vision from Lord Of The Rings. I dropped to the ground and sat gazing at it for a while. From the green tufts of vegetation around it the grey stone rose up like an impossible image of defiance to the laws of physics. I had seen countless images of it on the internet, but now seeing it before me I realised what an astonishing monument it was to men's desire to offer everything to God. It was also a huge relief to know I had survived the journey. I checked the time one last time and realised that it had taken me over four and a half hours to get here, and with the hour from Xeropotamou I had been walking for nearly six.

I climbed to my feet and stumbled down the last stretch of road, all the time aware of the monastery coming closer. I unfolded my cassock and wore it loosely around me so as to at least appear respectable. With about two hundred metres to go I spotted a figure in black chopping wood at the side of the road. As I approached he stopped work and greeted me in Greek. His clothes were torn and old, his grey beard a tangle around his face. He was the epitome of every Athonite monk I had had ever read about. Discovering my nationality he revealed he had a good grasp of English.

"Are you staying with us at the monastery?" He asked.

"No, I'm going on to Saint Grigoriou."

He seemed interested in talking, something I would have welcomed more than anything the previous day, or indeed any day before that. But now I was in no fit state to have a conversation. I tried to be polite but knew I had to get to water. He asked for a blessing and without thinking about it I obliged and was off.

Before the white walls of the main structure was a small courtyard where two Greek pilgrims sat chatting. At the sight of me they became quite alarmed and one of them offered to take my bag. I didn't have the strength to lift it from my shoulders and asked where the nearest tap was. They led me to a beautiful stone sink and from it flowed the coldest and sweetest water on earth. I drank from a metal cup chained to the wall and then slowly splashed water into my face. The contrast of temperatures brought home to me how burned my skin was. But with more water the heat and the miles disappeared, and I sat back against the cool stone wall grateful to the Theotokos for bringing me safely to this place.

After a few minutes recuperation I found the pilgrims again and asked them for directions to Saint Grigoriou. They told me they had come from there themselves and that it was just an hour and a half along the coast. They gave me rough directions and warned about the steep cliffs beside the pathway. I suspected they were only saying this because I looked so tired and so paid little attention.

I gave myself ten minutes rest and refilled both water bottles. Taking a final drink from the metal cup I followed their directions and started the descent to the sea about two hundred metres beneath the monastery. The path took me between some of the buildings of Simonos Petra along a narrow cobbled lane. Above me were wooden balconies along the beams of which twisted stunning green vines. Everything gave the impression of good order, that great attention had been applied to maintaining everything in the best condition it could be in.

The path then cut right towards the sea and I found myself overlooking terraces full of carefully regimented vegetable gardens. A single monk was tending the plants and I stopped to watch him for a few minutes. From this side of the monastery I could see enormous scaffolding clinging to the bleached stone, and I pitied whoever had to risk their life to work on such a precarious platform.

A few feet away a cat cried for attention and I found a pair of gentle blue eyes looking up at me. I resisted the impulse to stroke him knowing that a couple of deep scratches would be a bad addition to the day. He trustingly rolled on his back and my thoughts turned once more to my wife's instructions to photograph the cats. I said goodbye to him in the kind of soft voice even Greek cats can understand.

The path made a sudden and steep descent and once again I found walking with the aid of gravity a real pleasure. The route took me beneath a wooden structure that was laden with fruit. Some of it hung easily within reach but I knew it would be a terrible abuse of the monastery's hospitality to help myself to their food.

I continued to follow the path down into bushes that created a dense shadow and a brief hiding place from the sun. Within the undergrowth there was an ancient hermitage long since abandoned. It was half dug into the hill, half created by the spoil from the digging. I couldn't begin to imagine the austerity of such a life. The vegetation grew thicker as I walked and by the time I reached the sea there were large trees on either side of the path.

The monastery jetty was a stone structure jutting far enough out into the sea to allow quite large ferries to dock. I looked down into the water and despite its clarity couldn't see the sea bottom. I enjoyed the breeze blowing in from the Aegean for a while and then began my search for the path to Grigoriou.

The men had said the path went along the coastline, so I climbed over the first of the rocks to see if it was visible on the shore beyond them. To my confusion all that was visible was thick undergrowth and steep banks that were clearly impossible to climb. The more I looked the more I became frustrated as I realised I must have walked past the path on my descent. The frustration was not so much in having missed it but at the thought of having to climb back towards the monastery. This time gravity would be against me. I became annoyed with myself and knew there was nothing to be done but start the climb. It was steeper than I had noticed and after about twenty minutes the effects of the earlier hours of sunshine began to take their toll once again. I kept checking every break in the bushes in case it was the path but there was no sign of it. Eventually I was almost back to the monastery itself when I spotted a narrow cutting through the trees. There was no real indication that this was the route and I became a little resentful over it.

The warning about the cliffs had been warranted. As soon as I left the main path I immediately found myself picking my way over rocks with a fifty or sixty foot sheer drop to my left. The weight of my bag shifted dangerously each time I had to take a long step and I forced myself to move as slowly and deliberately as I could. The path cut back away from the cliff slightly and then descended into the dry valley I had been looking out across. There were steps dug into the ground which made walking easier and were also a reassurance that this was the right way. As I reached the very bottom I could see another skete on the hill. Somehow the inhabitants had created a small oasis of vegetables around their home and it struck me how powerful human activity could be in transforming the environment. Anything seemed possible with enough hard work.

Once across the narrow valley floor I began to climb again. At first there was plenty of shade but after about a half hour I was once again exposed to the sun. The full effects of my earlier walk began to make themselves known. Despite being rehydrated I was cooking. I climbed for about an hour and decided I had to lie down. There was no shade to be found so I lay under a low bush and took what I could. It occurred to me that maybe the hour and a half I was expecting was as inaccurate as the two hours I had previously been told about had proved to be. I had been lying like this for just a couple of minutes when I heard voices. I twisted my neck to discover three Germans standing over me. They looked extremely alarmed at the sight before them until I smiled and wished them good morning.

"Are you alright Father?"

"Yes, yes," I assured them, "how much further is it to the monastery?"

"About twenty minutes, a little more climbing and then you head downhill."

I thanked them for the information and they set off. I gave myself another five minutes rest and then pulled myself to my feet. The thought of being so close gave me an added determination and all the time I prayed to the Theotokos.

The path came out onto a level area that showed the first signs of cultivation. I knew I was getting closer. There was a sign declaring M. Ossiou Gregoriou and a hand painted arrow showing the way. I increased my pace and found myself on a dusty road that was marked with tyre tracks. I could now see the sea again and my expectation grew. Turning a final corner I found myself looking down on the red tiled roof of the eight-storey monastery. The buildings formed an S as they followed the contours of the cliff. Tall poplar trees stood elegantly beside the outer walls and a few smaller buildings were scattered across the hill immediately behind the main structure. But by now I was so exhausted that I felt no joy, only relief. I was walking with a comical gait trying to stop my legs from becoming raw and everything I was wearing was drenched in sweat. In this ridiculous condition I slowly made my way down the road to Gregoriou.

"Just as painters working from models constantly gaze at their exemplar and thus strive to transfer the expression of the original to their own artistry, so too he who is anxious to make himself perfect in all kinds
of virtue must gaze upon the lives of the saints and must make their excellence his own by imitation."

- Saint Basil The Great.

Chapter Eight

The monastery of Osiou Grigoriou gives the impression of being much smaller than it actually is. Much of its height stretches down over the edge of the cliff, giving the impression that it consists of a maximum of two storeys. In fact it has eight floors each of which has its own wooden balcony hanging out over the sea. Beneath these floors are further white walls dotted with the odd window. The buildings surround an open square and as I walked into it I was struck by the contrast of both the look and atmosphere of the place with what I had seen at Xeropotamou. Here there were monks everywhere; some chatting with pilgrims others busy organising workmen.

I approached one of the monks and asked for the guest master. He met me with a broad smile and pointed to the first balcony above me.

"Go to the end of the balcony and knock on the door," he said in a thick Greek accent. I thanked him and followed his directions. My legs were in a pretty bad shape by now and my progress up the stairs was slow. Along the balcony were long wooden benches and I dropped my bag on to the one nearest the door before knocking. An old, tall monk appeared and seeing my condition he immediately told me to sit. He brought me a cup of water from a sink at the end of the balcony and I gratefully received it.

"Have you eaten Father?" He asked.

"I had breakfast this morning."

"You must go into the kitchen," he pointed to a door across the square, "there is plenty of bread and fruit for visitors. I will arrange your room Father, when you have eaten wait for me here." With that he fetched a door key from his room and strode off along the balcony to prepare things for me. I reluctantly climbed to my feet again and wandered over to the kitchen. It was a large room full of stainless steel: but no bread. It was reminiscent of a school kitchen. I could see from the crumbs in a large bowl where bread had been and wondered if I was to look elsewhere. I searched the tops but there was nothing. Ordinarily I would have left it at that as I wasn't particularly hungry anyway, but the effects of the sun meant I wasn't thinking clearly. I pulled open a cupboard to see if the bread was sitting in there but still no luck.

As I was doing this a monk entered the far end of the kitchen and began to scream at me. A torrent of impenetrable Greek poured out of him as he rushed towards me.

"The father told me I would find some bread," I tried to explain. But his shouting in Greek didn't stop. He took me by the arm and forcefully led me out of the kitchen. As we emerged into the square a few heads turned to see what was causing the commotion. Nothing I said in English was helping the situation so I strolled back to my place on the balcony. From there I could see the monk still loudly explaining what had happened to a second monk, he was wildly gesturing with his arms and throwing me the occasional glance as he spoke. I had clearly made a terrible impression and wondered if I was going to be asked to leave. I was too tired to feel any concern, and sat quite passively watching the scene and waiting for whatever would happen next.

The loud monk eventually went back to his kitchen and I sensed things wouldn't develop into anything serious. I was becoming tired of the errors I was making and felt a little miserable. The guestmaster returned and asked if I had eaten.

"No, I couldn't see any bread. I'm afraid the monk in the kitchen wasn't very happy with me being in there."

At this he looked across at the kitchen with such annoyance that I had a strong feeling of his genuine concern for me. It lifted my spirits.

"Please follow me Father, your room is ready." He then lifted my bag which had been sitting on the bench where I had originally left it and slipped it over his shoulder.

We turned directly off the balcony along a corridor of guest-rooms. He opened the door for me and handed me a large iron key.

"Vespers is in half an hour Father." I thanked him and he was gone. Once again as a priest I had been honoured with a room to myself and so had the choice of three immaculately arranged single beds. And once again there was a pair of slippers beneath each. Outside the window I could hear a couple of pilgrims chatting, they were sitting on one of the wooden balconies over the sea. I took out a change of shirt and my toiletries and went off to find the bathroom.

Standing in front of the sink I got my first look at myself in a mirror since I had been on Athos: it was not a good sight. My entire face had darkened considerably and the exertion had left my eyes looking sunken and red. I tried to repair the damage with plenty of water and then headed back to my room. Stretching out on the bed I felt the restorative power of rest working in my limbs.

The half hour went quickly but it was enough. I walked over to the church eager for the first service. Once again I was wary of taking a place uninvited at the front of the church. The building was arranged just as it had been at Xeropotamou, with a series of rooms and walls of icons leading to the actual iconostasis. Before the service began a monk collected me and led me to a stall with the choir.

The monks around me were much younger than I expected. Many of them looked to be in their late twenties or early thirties. There was a much more relaxed feeling amongst them than I had previously seen, and also many more of them. The singing began in the usual pattern of call and response from one side of the church to the other, but the method of conducting the service was unusual. A monk had responsibility for providing the right books and finding the correct pages while the choir simply sang what was placed in front of them. This meant they were free to focus entirely on the singing and not be distracted with hunting around for the next line.

The two young monks standing next to me were involved in a private joke and it relaxed me enormously to see them chuckling to themselves. The anxieties I had allowed to develop inside me as a result of reading so many misinformed books were entirely misplaced. There was no sense of judgement over matters of "correctness" in minor things. I had worried that I wouldn't know what to do or how to conduct myself in church, but as it happened this was the one place where I felt secure and error free.

The singing carried me into a state of prayer very quickly and the day's physical exertion stripped me of any romantic notions of where I was or what was taking place. My mind was cleared of distractions and I was able to focus entirely on God. Again I was invited to venerate the icons at the head of the line of monks and I gratefully did so

101

with a powerful sense of joy in my heart. As the service ended I knew it had been the right thing to make the walk, God had used the day to prepare me for the worship. The demands on my body had put me in the right frame of mind to be there and I instinctively understood that God had blessed me.

The church door led directly to the refectory and we walked in between the tables already set out for dinner. A monk invited me forward and showed me to the table immediately beside that of the abbot. We stood at our places until he entered, prayed the blessing and then together we all sat and started eating.

The dishes of food had been laid out in advance. They consisted of a mushroom and pasta dish and very large amounts of vegetables, fruit and olives. Each person had a whole cucumber before them. I sliced mine up into the main dish and relished every spoonful. The home grown and chemical-free produce was delicious, and after eating I was extremely full. I had read in countless books about the regime at mealtimes on Athos but again the reality was different. I expected to be eating in silence while a suitable text was read aloud but instead a few monks whispered conversations and there was no reading. It was the first opportunity to get an idea of how many monks were in the monastery and I realised that every table in what was a good sized room was full. My earlier impression of their ages was confirmed: there were many monks here younger than myself, their black beards showing not a hint of grey.

After the meal a priest stood at the door and each man received a blessing from him as they left the refectory. As I stepped out into the sunshine an older monk with a pure white beard that nearly reached his waist approached me.

"Father, have you come from England?" His accent carried a hint of southern England.

"Yes," I said, a little surprised.

"Please," he continued, "would you like to sit and talk?"

"Thank you Father," I replied. We sat on the ledge of a low wall shaded by the building behind us.

"Are you from England?" I asked.

"Yes, my parents are Greek but I was born in London. I grew up in North London and went to school there. They will be bringing out the monastery's relics for pilgrims to venerate soon. After that would you like to come and have tea with me and talk?"

"Very much Father." At that moment I could think of nothing I wanted more.

"When you have finished, I will come and find you. See you in a while." He stood and smiled before walking off towards an arched doorway in the corner of the square.

I noticed the few pilgrims who were present were now heading towards the church again and so I joined them. The priest who had blessed us after dinner was now standing behind a table in front of the Royal Doors. He waited for everyone to gather around him and then began his identification of the many relics laid out before us. He did so in Greek and then repeated the whole thing in English.

"This is a part of the True Cross; this is the right hand of Anastasia the Roman; this is the skull of Saint Gregory Nazianzes, the father of Saint Gregory the Theologian; this is a bone from Saint Dionysios and these bones are from Saints Cosmas and Damian."

He raised his hand to indicate that I should come first and so I worked my way along the table, bowing and making the sign of the cross to honour these holy saints as I carefully kissed each one.

When the last pilgrim had finished I offered the priest my payer rope and he blessed it on each of the holy relics. He then walked over to a large and beautiful icon.

"This is the miraculous icon called the Virgin Pantanassa, it has survived many fires unharmed." We each venerated the icon as we had the relics. The priest continued his talk.

"The monastery is dedicated to Saint Nicholas; it was founded in the fourteenth century by Saint Gregory of Sinai whose typicon is still in use here today." He then turned back to the table and was joined by another monk who helped carry the relics to safety behind the iconostasis.

Outside I spotted the Russian priest from the ferry waiting near the guestmaster's room. We smiled and acknowledged each other with the customary half bow. I went back to my room and was about to lie down when there was a light knocking at the door: it was the monk from England.

"Would you like to come to my workshop? We can have tea on the balcony."

I followed him across the courtyard where he unlocked the heavy old door beneath the archway. Inside he proudly showed off his workspace and explained his obedience. I will avoid describing in detail his work for fear of identifying him without his permission. He then opened a second door and told me to sit out on the balcony while he made the tea. He had a couple of plastic garden chairs and a matching table on the small wooden balcony. I looked down over the ledge to see the crystal clear water lapping at the rocks. The evening sky was cloudless, a picture of serenity. I took my seat and looked out at the horizon where a distant boat was slowly making its way east.

"Man can attain to holiness only in God, not by nature, but by participation, by struggle, by prayer."

-Saint Cyril of Jerusalem.

Chapter Nine

He brought out a tray and laid it before me. Green tea without milk that at first was too bitter but with each sip I grew closer to acquiring the taste for.

"This is a stunning view you have, it's a wonder you can get any work done at all."

He laughed. "I do like to sit out here, though there are too many midges this year."

"They never bite me," I observed, and he explained about the hormones released by certain people through the skin that attract insects.

"The humidity is also changing," he said, looking out at the sea. "About ten years ago the summers here were much fresher, but especially over the last five years there has been an increase in humidity."

"Is that related to global warming?"

"Something like that, global climate change at any rate."

"You sound like you're sceptical," I said.

"A few years ago they were talking about the green house effect. Have you noticed they've dropped that phrase? For now it's global warming, there'll be another name for it before long."

"But if the climate is changing then it must be real," I suggested.

"If you look at the figures I think they point more to the possibility of a coming ice age rather then warming. It's definitely changing though. There was one of the fathers here at the monastery when I arrived who could look at the skies in October and November and every year he would forecast the winter's weather exactly through to January and February. He was so closely attuned to the skies that he could read them perfectly. For the last three or four years he has been unable to do so. They have lost their natural pattern – or at least the pattern that existed before. There are changes for sure, but don't be fooled by government explanations" He studied my face for a moment.

"I'm not sure what you mean," I admitted.

"The carbon taxes that are being talked about will be the first international taxes to cover the entire developed world. These taxes are really what it's all about. There is a global push for increased taxes; the ultimate goal is to reduce the power and wealth of the middle classes."

This struck me as quite a statement to make, "For what purposes?" I asked.

"The drive is Luciferian," he explained. "There are power elites in the world working towards their final end game."

"Do you mean one world government?" I had recently read an article about this online and was interested to hear his perspective.

"Yes, the organisations that control the world banking systems are moving in one direction. Did you know that almost all national banks are actually privately owned? The decisions about interest rates are made by private banking groups who work for their own purposes, not the public's. And certainly not the interest of nations. The modern banking system is a dangerous tool that the wrong people have taken control of."

"But why would they want to reduce the standing of the middle classes?" I asked.

"The middle classes are educated; they are always a problem for these kinds of people. They ask difficult questions and expect to be treated fairly." He smiled at this.

"When you say Lucifarian, do you mean it is working towards Antichrist?"

"Oh yes, that is certainly true. We are living in the end times for sure; we just don't know which chapter we're in."

"But what about the signs that we are told to look for?"

"Look around you," he said calmly, "the world is moving towards a one world government as never before. The destruction of Greece as a political and cultural entity has been a goal for some years. Because it is the destruction of Christian culture that is actually necessary and this cannot happen so long as the Greek people hold true to their customs. Look at the education system, the destruction of families, the acceleration in the promotion of anti-

Christian values and morals: the signs are there for those who will look."

"But what about the rebuilding of the temple in Jerusalem? Is that to be taken as a literal thing?" I asked.

"The fathers believe it is a literal thing. But the Jews are preparing for this even today. For the first time since AD 70 they are training the temple priests, they are making the vestments. There are some very powerful people who believe that it will not be long before it comes about. But I can see you are concerned when I talk about the Jews. The real problem isn't Jews it is Zionists, and there are more American Protestant Zionists than Jewish ones."

"But there's a problem for them," I smiled, "there's a big golden dome on the Temple Mount."

"The conflict with Islam is part of the plan," he explained. "Long ago the plan for three world wars was prepared, and the final one will be seen as a religious war. Of course, in reality it will be no more about religion than any of the previous wars were about the things people were told they were about. The control and supply of information is perhaps easier now than it has ever been before. People believe what they are told, especially if they are poorly educated. Our children leave school arrogant, convinced that they are something special, schools work to inflate their self-esteem, but they come out knowing very little and understanding even less."

I nodded slowly as I tried to take in his words. In response to my frown he said "You must pray for the world. Encourage your people to pray for the whole world. It is more important now than ever before."

As he was talking the light had faded and now we could only see one another as vague outlines. This added emphasis to his words as his voice emerged from the shadows.

"We are living in a time when most people in the west have no idea how the world is run or what is happening around them. Their working hours are being stretched, their wages reduced in comparison to inflation, they are being forced into a new kind of slavery, in fact a slavery that is very old indeed. People are losing touch with the most basic things because their lives are being made so unnatural." He paused a moment as if to allow me to absorb what he was saying. "It isn't natural for man to work every hour and lose touch with his family. Children are growing up in households where parents are becoming distant figures. And the rule of television means even the free time that is available is given away to sitting motionless in front of the box. This is partly why there is a rise in the moral sickness that we see about us. Homosexuality, drugs, people are turning to whatever makes them feel good because they are lost in this unnatural state."

"But what can we do about it," I asked, "I mean, not just for ourselves but for other people?"

"You must pray," he repeated. "You must try to live an authentically Christian life. Do you understand what I mean by this?"

"I'm not sure," I admitted.

"The Christian west, in fact western civilisation as a whole has lost touch with true Christianity. It proclaims Christian words, but it no longer has any real grasp of authentic Christianity. A full thousand years now separates the west from true Christianity, from the tradition of the Church. It is so polluted with nihilism that what it believes to be Christianity is really an empty shell. The Church has always proclaimed that we are not here simply to be blessed by God with particular gifts or experiences; but that we are created to become gods by grace. Our Creator is God by nature but we are called to be gods by grace. Western Christians believe that the purpose of their faith is moral improvement or the hope of heaven one day. Yes we must work to become more moral, but this is not the goal, it is part of the process. The west no longer understands that our purpose in life is Theosis. Do you understand that word?"

I nodded, the word was known to me but this way of describing it was not.

"The whole theology of the west has become focussed on atonement theories, seeing the incarnation only in terms of sacrifice, the death of Christ on the cross. But the Church has always understood the incarnation to be the means by which our humanity is raised in Christ. Adam and Eve desired to become like God through their own

111

will, their own scheme because they were deceived by Satan. In fact God's way is that we become gods through humility, through obedience and love. The communion of Paradise was broken by sin, but Christ establishes a new communion in and through Himself. The two natures of God and man in Christ establish a new communion for all men. Human nature is now enthroned in Christ in heaven. Modern western man sees himself as no more than an animal, an evolved ape; he languishes in this bestial state. Once again Satan's deception is at work. The Church has always understood that now nothing can separate us from God because our nature, our humanity is enthroned in the bosom of the Holy Trinity. And how did God descend to earth? Through the Theotokos. She is the link, the bridge between heaven and earth. Without her willingness to participate in God's plan the incarnation could not have happened. This is why we venerate her. And when we enter a church we see not only Christ's mother but all the saints too. Our icons declare the reality of those people who have been known to be changed into the likeness of Christ. They confirm to us the truth of Christ's promises. They are a living witness to the reality of Theosis that we must all find in our lives."

I sat quietly, listening to each word with a heart that was filling with joy. As he spoke I knew I understood what I had so often skirted around. His words came gently but with real power. He didn't rush but there was an energy in his speech that gave his message force.

"Many in the west who seek God imagine they must do it alone through their moral transformation. But the Church is not an invisible or moral grouping; it is the real, identifiable Church. We are deified as the Body of Christ through the sacramental life of the Church in the power of the Holy Spirit. The Church is the one and only place where man may be deified. It is the only source of God's sacramental grace. And any claims by other Christian groups to share in this grace are false. There is One Church, the Orthodox Church is the Church of the Apostles, the two are identical, there is no other Church outside of Orthodoxy. The energies of God are at work in The Church; He has entered His creation and now He deifies us through those same energies. Created in God's image and likeness we all yearn for union with God and only through the life of Orthodoxy is this possible. And put simply, the life of Orthodoxy is the recognition of our spiritual sickness and the healing of this through repentance and grace. Western man is desperate to be in control of his life, to feel he can trust in what he has achieved or built. But the Church teaches us to let go of any such assurances, to recognise our weakness and need for God. When we are humble and truly recognise our dependence on God alone we are moving towards Theosis. But this requires some struggle. Life here on the Holy Mountain is about subduing the unnatural desires and urges of the flesh and mind. It is an arena in which the monk trains himself to be humble and renounce self-will and self-reliance. Selfishness must be overcome with a certain amount of asceticism. The passions must be subdued before we can discover true freedom. So long as we follow our own desires we are slaves to the passions though western man imagines this slavery to be freedom. Satan convinces him that man alone must rule because he has no higher god."

He had stopped talking and I hadn't noticed. I was so caught up in his words that my mind was still busy in the silence. I sensed it was late and knew that we had to be up for four a.m..

"Father, you have been so generous with your time, but it's late and I must let you get some sleep."

"We will continue in the morning after breakfast," he promised.

"Thank you, I would like that very much."

The dividing line between sea and sky was now lost in the darkness. It looked like the black sky stretched down to the very foot of the cliffs beneath us. We stood and he led me through the workshop.

"Thank you again," I said.

"I will see you in the morning, sleep well." He turned and was gone.

I returned to my room as quietly as I could. There wasn't a sign of anyone else still awake. I made the sign of the cross and lay down over the sheets, my mind clear and at peace. I checked my alarm clock and found I had five hours before I had to be up. My body was desperate to make up for the hours of walking and without any difficulty I fell quickly to sleep.

"The more you pray and entreat God for your sins the more the evil demons withdraw from you, while the more you neglect prayer and lack the desire to pray, the more they approach you and you become their dwelling place."

- Elder Gabriel Dionysiatis

Chapter Ten

The alarm woke me at three-thirty a.m.. I lay still for a minute absorbing the reality of where I was. Any tiredness quickly left me as I thought about the service to come. Somewhere in the dark a lone monk began beating the symantron and I thought of the monks being called to prayer, of the many faces coming to life in the simple cells scattered around the monastery. For me it was all new, but they were climbing from their bunks as they always did and as they would until the day they died. As the beating of the wood called for Christians to meet with God I realised how the lack of bells was a reminder of how little security there could be for us in this world. Forced to hit wood on wood the Church in this part of the world had even been denied something as simple as bells. The sound of the symantron was a warning not to take anything for granted, that the world is full of powers and people opposed to the freedoms we sometimes do

116

not even understand as freedoms. Unlike the previous night when I had felt a certain excitement to hear the sound, it now seemed extremely sober and removed any silly romantic notions I had developed about it.

I dressed and quickly visited the washroom. As I made my way to the church door I joined a small group of monks as they entered. Following them in I was able to copy whatever they did and felt relaxed about not doing the wrong thing. We venerated the icons on the walls of each room as we passed through to the iconostasis. This movement between chambers created a sense of drawing closer to the holy table, and the physical space communicated a mysterious reality that was very strong but not something I could have articulated in rational terms. It was very dark as there were only a few candles burning and as I peered into the shadows trying to decide where I should stand a monk appeared at my side and guided me to the right stall. Once again they had positioned me next to the choir to the left of the Royal Doors. There was silence for a few minutes as more figures in black entered and I found myself standing with a group of about a dozen monks, all of whom except one were under the age of forty. Their thick black beards and youthful faces made a powerful impression on me.

A number of candles were lit in front of the icons and from the high ceiling an oil lamp suspended by a long chain dropped down to head height at incredible speed. The monk controlling it managed to do it with such skill that at the last moment he slowed and then stopped it before it jerked or shook loose. He appeared beside it to light it and received an approving nod from one of the other young monks. Once the lamp was burning he then raised it and repeated the action on the other side of the church. This process was repeated throughout the night at key moments in the service and each time its rapid descent was controlled in a way that conveyed the joy of performing such a small function.

The two groups of monks forming the choir had now arranged themselves around their book stands on opposite sides of the church. A monk who was well over six foot five standing in the stall next to me began to lead the chants. His voice was deep and steady and I could see the others looking to his lead. Their singing blended into a beautiful range of tones and textures, a sound that can only be produced by people who spend many hours singing together. There was no strain or excessive force, but the power of their chants was like thunder: it was clear that they were singing on behalf of the whole world. The Greek language takes on a special beauty when it is used to sing to God. This is true of all human languages of course, as this is the ultimate purpose of all words. But chants written and sung over so many centuries find their natural expression in Greek that flows and fits so perfectly around the holy expressions of worship.

Just as in the first night's service I found my own lack of Greek wasn't a problem. The atmosphere of devotion carried me along and I found myself praying very easily. As the light began to find its way through the windows I felt I never wanted to leave. Being there created the feeling that there was nowhere else on earth to be and nothing more to do than to pray. It was an utterly complete feeling and I could only begin to imagine what it did to a man to spend years here knowing that there would be nothing else. It is the sense of eternity breaking into the limits of created time through the repeated words and actions of prayer.

A wave of gratitude swept over me as I realised how generous it was that they should allow outsiders to wander in and taste even the tiniest morsel of their feast. A stream of visitors, constant new faces, must have some impact on their lives. And yet they manage to continue as though each pilgrim had always been there. And more than that, they manage to make pilgrims feel welcome and honour them with their hospitality. At times I caught myself looking at the faces around me and had to consciously pull my gaze away. But it was difficult because in them I could see holiness. Their dark eyes were humbly lowered, full of gentleness and peace. It hardly seemed possible that there could be so many men in this generation who would devote their lives so completely to seeking union with God. How little of my own life in comparison was truly devoted to God. The endless worries and concerns of life in the world were an illusion, a distraction from the true purpose of existence. Although I knew God had not called me to live like these men, I understood that by being with them I was able to understand my own life with a greater clarity. Simply being in the presence of holy activities has a profound effect on us: how much more it must be to live it.

As I turned I realised that in the stall to my right was the Russian priest from the ferry. We smiled our acknowledgements of one another again and nodded our hellos. As the service moved on it was reassuring to have another priest who was as unsure as myself about what he should be doing. But this was never any kind of problem. The atmosphere was relaxed, one of complete acceptance. At no time did I worry that I wasn't prostrating properly or doing something I shouldn't. Amongst the monks I even saw a couple of moments of levity and caught a couple of them chuckling over a shared joke. The older monk who was finding and delivering the right pages for them to sing out of feigned a stern frown to which they smiled broadly. The reality of their brotherhood and love was unmistakeable.

At the end of the Liturgy the Russian and I were invited forward and together we venerated the holy images. This was something we had both done many times in our own parish churches thousands of miles apart but as we did it together there was nothing that separated us. The faith for all people united us completely. The image of the Theotokos before us evoked the same veneration, the same thankfulness regardless of culture and nationality. We walked together through the laymen at the back of the church waiting to be come forward and out into the monastery square.

"How has your visit been going?" He asked.

"A real blessing," I said, deciding not to recount my adventures walking on the mountain.

"Have you had an opportunity to talk with any of the monks?" He continued.

"Yes, in fact I'm meeting with Father X after breakfast. What about you?"

"It has been a good trip; I have much to take back with me." He pointed to a low wall. "Shall we sit?"

We found a spot shaded from the early morning sun.

"Do you have a large parish in Russia?"

"Oh yes, we are in the South of Moscow. We have four priests serving in our church."

"Is that because you have so many people to care for?"

"There has been a huge increase in numbers these last fifteen years. When we celebrate the Divine Liturgy there is always a priest who hears confessions. We take it in turns, and for the whole morning we will do nothing but hear people confess. Hundreds of people each day will come for this."

"Is it the same right across Russia or just in the cities?"

"Yes, all over Russia the Church is growing. Many men are offering themselves for the priesthood. Churches are being built and people are filling them. For the older faithful this is a wondrous thing after so many years of persecution.

I am thirty-six and had to be baptised in secret. My mother lived outside Moscow and had to take me on a train into the city where a priest received me into the Church. If she had been caught the authorities would have punished both her and the priest. This is the way it was for a long time. But now we are baptising openly and the people are free to come."

I had read accounts of such things but hearing a man speak of his living experience and the dangers his family had faced for their faith was very moving.

"How is the Church in England?" He asked.

"It is growing, but nothing like you describe in Russia." I admitted. "Orthodoxy is still unknown to many people, but there are new communities starting across the country. Many people are converting from Anglicanism, but there are also lots of immigrants from Romania, Russia, Serbia and so on."

"And what language do you worship in?" He asked.

"English," I smiled, "we have a very good translation of the services."

He nodded approval at this, "There are even some Russians who do not understand all of the Liturgy in Russia, I think it is good that you use the language people can speak."

As we chatted a few of the monks appeared from the church, but instead of entering the refectory they began to move out through large monastery gates towards the dock. One of them approached us and said "We have a bishop visiting, please fathers, come and join us to welcome him."

We followed him out and joined the line of monks waiting to greet the visitor who was climbing the steps from his boat. With him was a black deacon, only the second black face I had seen on Athos, who looked to be in his early twenties. The bishop was rather portly in comparison with the monks, his long white beard waving in the breeze. As he passed the line of men he blessed them and each kissed his hand. When he reached us he stopped and began speaking in Greek. I explained that I was English and he asked "Where in England have you come from Father?"

"Herefordshire," I said.

"It is good to have English Orthodox visiting the Holy Mountain, who is your bishop?"

"Archbishop Gregorios," I said.

"Ah yes, very good," and with that he blessed me. I kissed his hand and the abbot led him away. The line of monks followed on behind and as we entered the courtyard I could see that we were returning to the church. Inside the singing had already begun and even before I could see him, I knew it was the black deacon's voice. He was chanting in Greek but his African accent and tone were unmistakeable. The bishop responded and it was clear how pleased the community was to receive him.

After a short twenty minutes of prayer we were invited to receive a further Episcopal blessing and then we made our way to breakfast. The monks stood silently at the tables and the Russian priest and I were led to one immediately beside the bishop's. He was led in and with great solemnity he blessed the food. We took our seats on the long benches and began to eat. There were bowls of rice mixed with mushrooms and peppers and once again everyone had an entire cucumber before them. I was a little uncertain about whether I could eat the whole thing for breakfast but managed to slice it up and mix it in with the main dish. There were also jugs of both water and wine before us and lots of olives. Unlike the previous night, everyone ate in silence and the abbot climbed what looked like an Anglican pulpit from where he carefully read to us. I didn't know if this was the usual custom at breakfast or if they were taking care to satisfy the bishop's expectations. The cucumber turned out to be almost crispy it was so fresh and I found the food very satisfying.

The bishop's deacon began to set up a microphone on a small stand in front of him and then produced a recording device that he plugged it into. Satisfied that it was ready the bishop then banged three times on the table with his spoon. Everyone stopped eating and there was complete silence. He gave a speech in Greek that was clearly heartfelt. Even though the meaning of the words was lost to me I could feel his emotions as he expressed his obvious pleasure in being there.

When he finished speaking the tall monk from church moved to the back of the room and the members of the choir joined him. There they began to sing in the bishop's honour and again he was clearly moved. As they brought their chants to an end everyone stood and a path appeared between the rows of monks as they parted to make way for the bishop. With great warmth the abbot accompanied him having had no breakfast himself and we followed on behind.

The sunshine was now back to its intense brightness and I looked around for some shade. Before I could move to it the monk who had given me so much of his time the night before approached me.

"Father," he said, "we must finish our conversation. Would you like to join me on the terrace?"

"Yes, thank you," I couldn't have been happier.

He led me through the same arched doorway and through his workshop.

"Please Father, take a seat while I prepare some tea."

I stepped out onto the little wooden balcony and looked down at the sea beneath me. There schools of various kinds of fish were rising and diving in the water. Some of them looked large even from a distance and I realised how so many of the hermits I had read about managed to feed themselves living in tiny settlements perched so precariously on the cliffs.

The monk emerged with his tray and placed two cups on the little plastic table. I admired the fish and he said "There used to be many more. Even in my time here I have seen a reduction in the numbers and the size. The seas are being far more heavily fished and the effects are dramatic."

"Do you get many bishops visiting?" I enquired.

"Not really, the bishop you met this morning was once a monk here at Grigoriou. A few years ago he was given the obedience of supporting a mission in Africa. When the bishop at the time died he was chosen to replace him. It brings great joy to the whole community when he is able to return, and I am sure it is important for him too."

"Do many of the monks from Athos become bishops?"

He nodded. "A good number have gone out into the world to serve in this way. This is a hard demand to make on the individual men, which is to give up their life here on the Holy Mountain. But the Church needs wise bishops. Too often the Church imagines that a university education is sufficient to qualify a man for such high office. In fact I would say that studying in western universities is the last thing that our shepherds need. Modern theological schools are deeply affected by the humanistic thinking of the world. Many have tried to achieve acceptance by secular groups by introducing modern ideas of how the Bible should be read or how theology should be interpreted. All of these things will only lead people away from the truth."

I began to think of my own experience at theological college and understood only too well what he meant.

"The mind is very easily misled," he continued. "All of us, including the fathers on Athos, must struggle to free ourselves from false images. We carry within us illusions about everything. Saint John Chrysostom taught that we are blinded by false images of everything. First we fail to see ourselves clearly because we do not see our true spiritual state. Pride clouds our judgement and we live with fantasies of who and what we are. This prevents us from seeking true repentance because we are unable to know what it is that needs healing within us.

Secondly we fail to see one another because we have developed distorted pictures of other human beings. We are taught to treat each other as rivals, or as threats, or as objects to satisfy our own desires. Do you suppose we could really be so cruel and unloving if we could see the true humanity of one another?"

I shook my head in response to his rhetorical question.

"And of course, we carry false ideas about God. This is perhaps the greatest danger of all. There are many people who have been taught to see God as an angry judge and quite naturally they find it impossible to learn to love Him. But we must love Him. We can never be what we were created to be if we fail to love God. Not just believe in Him as the demons do, in fear, but truly love Him for all He is and all He has done for us. From an early age God was used by different people as a means to getting their way. History is full of powerful people who have pronounced the will of God in such a way as to further their own ends. And so people learn to resent what they believe oppresses them. But God oppresses nobody. We must strip away the illusions we carry about God in order to meet Him as He is. This is the nature of Theosis that I was talking about last night. There are many people unwilling to do this for a range of reasons. It may be that it feels threatening to abandon long-held beliefs, or it may be too painful to face up to the truth of ourselves. But we must if we are to fulfil our purpose."

"How does this apply to non-Orthodox?" I asked.

"This applies to everyone." he said. "There are countless Orthodox people who refuse to face up to the truth of themselves or of God. In fact all of us, whether we are Orthodox or not, whether we are priests or monks or laymen, we must work hard to abandon falsehood. Ultimately this can only be done through a certain amount of ascetic struggle and prayer, because only when we meet God can we know Him. Western theology teaches that God can be known about like some object or scientific proof. But this is nonsense. Yes, the intellect must be offered to God, but we cannot truly know God simply by thinking about Him, however lofty our thoughts may be. The theology of the Church comes from God, it is revealed, it is not the product of man's desire to reach up to God. This is the Tower of Babel. We cannot build anything that captures God or His truth, we can only be obedient and repent and wait for Him to come to us if He so chooses."

I looked into the simplicity of his face that appeared utterly guileless from which was coming such depths of wisdom. As though in response to my thoughts he said

"Do you have a sense of why God has brought you to Athos?"

I paused for a moment, wondering if I would be able to find the right words. "I am having many experiences that are affecting me deeply."

"Yes, and they will go on revealing themselves to you long after you have left. The full meaning of conversations and encounters that you have here might seem hidden at first, but God blesses us here through the prayers of His Holy Mother. Do not disregard the most insignificant thing from your trip, God is in all things and is able to use all things for His purposes. If we can become alert to Him we find that even apparently accidental or painful experiences may be of great blessing to us if we are able to receive them in the right way."

"Please," I said, "could you explain a little about how we do this."

"It is simple and yet very difficult," he smiled. "If we struggle to become like Christ then everything can become a blessing because we accept everything as the will of God. While we are still clinging to our own will, insisting on what we think is best for us then we are resisting God's will, God's plan, and things feel painful or difficult. Even death may be seen this way. If we see anyone's death, including our own, in any way other than through the truth of the Resurrection, it can only be a catastrophe and tragedy. But for Christians there is victory in death because we know we shall be raised by God. The world can take many things from us, but it cannot take away our death!"

This astonishing statement hit me with great impact, and for a moment at least I felt released from any fear. He must have understood this from the look on my face because he then said something that I had never expected.

"There is no need of fear when we trust in God. I truly believe that anyone who calls on God, genuinely cries out to Him for help, will be saved."

I was slightly troubled by this, it sounded like universalism that went against much that I understood to be Church doctrine. Without wishing to contradict him, but genuinely wanting to know what he meant, I said "How can this be if you believe that only the sacraments of the Church are salvic?"

"Salvation!" He spoke the word as though it were an item laid out before us on the table to be gazed at. "What do you think is meant by salvation?"

"I suppose ultimately it is living with God eternally."

"You must remember that Christ also warned that there are many rooms in His Father's house."

I had only ever heard that verse used as a means of comfort, a reassurance that we must not assume anyone to be excluded from God's Kingdom. "I'm not sure what you mean," I said.

"God's mercy is beyond our imagining. The fathers teach us that all of our sins are like a teardrop in the ocean of God's mercy. But this is not to say that all will receive an equal reward. As we are able to receive, so God blesses us. This is the message of the talents. We must enter this process of Theosis in order to be blessed. But this does not mean that God will simply cast out those who have not yet begun that transformation. But also it does not mean that the high chambers of God's mansion will be a suitable place for them to live. This is figurative language because we cannot see fully into the mystery of eternity, but since Christ revealed this way of looking at it to us then it must be enough."

He went quiet for a moment to allow me to gather my thoughts. Then he asked "Is there anything you would like to talk about before you go?"

Again I gave myself a moment to think, and then said "Could you talk to me a little about The Jesus Prayer?"

"Yes, of course, do you say the Jesus Prayer?"

"Yes, I find it helps me to focus on God." I said.

"Indeed, and do you say it when the feeling takes you or do you use a prayer rope in a more structured way?"

"I do use a prayer rope just to help avoid distracting thoughts about time, but it's not a particularly structured thing." I admitted.

He thought for a moment and then said "The name of Jesus has great power. Spiritual power. There are some who have shortened the whole prayer just to the repetition of Christ's name. This is an extremely intense way of praying and not suitable for most people. But I mention it because it is a good indication of what is happening when we say the Jesus Prayer. We are communing with God and the simplicity of the repetition helps us to focus on God's presence with us. Over time there are those for whom the prayer descends down from the head to the heart where it can be felt operating. The Prayer finds a home in the heart and brings great consolation."

This description was familiar to me but it was not something I had ever experienced. As he spoke about *those* for whom this has happened I knew from the authorative way he was describing it that it was something he knew from direct experience.

"I find it easier to pray using the Jesus Prayer than liturgical forms of worship." As I said this it felt like a confession somehow.

"That is understandable, you have not been a priest for very long and for now you are still having to concentrate to get things right. With time you will be more confident about what you are doing and will be able to pray more freely."

"But if I'm honest," I said, "I don't find it anywhere near the same experience."

"That is because it is not the same experience," he smiled. "When a priest leads others in worship he must make a small sacrifice of his own spiritual

132

needs in order to enable others to meet theirs. But as you know, the grace of the priesthood brings with it many other blessings."

"For a couple of weeks after I was ordained," I told him, "I found prayer was very easy and I was filled with a sense of always wanting to run back to God at every opportunity. But then slowly the demands of my life started becoming bolder again."

"There is an old saying," he said, "when we are baptised, or ordained, we have ten angels praying with us. As they support us our spiritual life feels very rich and grace-filled. But as each day goes by an angel leaves us until at the end of ten days we are left with only our Guardian Angel to pray with us." He smiled again at the child-like nature of the truth in the story and I recognised how perfectly this described my experience.

"So long as we try to be obedient to God and repent when we fail to be obedient, our Guardian Angel will stay with us. You must pray to your angel and ask for him to pray for you."

"I will," I said, knowing that so few of my intercessions were given to my angel to pray with me. "Can you describe the effect the many hours you spend in church has on your private prayer?" I asked.

"Your question implies a kind of thinking that is mistaken. In practical terms there is, of course, a difference between the prayers I say in my cell and the prayers I say with the community in church. But in reality there is no difference, it is all part of a single act of worship that continues on whether we are painting icons, digging vegetables or chanting before the holy images. The goal here is to make everything that we do become an offering to God so that our lives and our very existence become an offering." He pursed his lips slightly and then admitted "I too find it easier to be aware of prayer when I am in silence saying the Jesus Prayer than in church sometimes, though I am not sure the abbot would be happy to hear me say that. But what we feel is not the true benchmark by which we should judge what we are doing. We are sinful and confused creatures and what we take as a comforting or enjoyable feeling may be the result of something that isn't necessarily the right thing for us. Prayers are more powerful when we have to make an effort, and we should remember that when our spiritual lives become a struggle this may actually be the time when we are progressing. Western thinking has placed too much emphasis on the individual's own sense of what is right. There is no humility in this. If we really understood our spiritual condition we would never trust ourselves in anything. Obedience is hardest where there is too much pride because the proud man believes he is right and knows what's best. This kind of over-confidence has led many people astray and is of the devil."

"In the world it is sometimes expected that we trust ourselves, in fact for many kinds of work it is demanded of people," I said.

"Yes," he said, "I do not discount what you are saying. But we are not talking here about giving up responsibility for our lives. If you have a job and a family you must make decisions that affect yourself and other people. In those situations you must draw on your experience and knowledge to try and do the right thing. But self-reliance and pride may prevent a man from seeking help or advice from others, it may cripple him when he has to admit things have gone wrong or that he doesn't know what to do. If we are obedient in all things we seek to be humble and forgiving to all. Obedience to God can be followed even when we are working to figure something out. It isn't the abandonment of our intellect." He smiled again, "I think we have returned to our earlier theme."

I smiled back and in a single gulp finished my tea that had gone cold.

"Thank you so much for giving me your time Father," I said rising to my feet. He stood and led me through his workshop once more.

"I have put a few articles and videos on a disc which relate to what we were talking about last night." He handed me a DVD that he must have sat up copying long after I had gone to be bed. I expressed my gratitude but at the time didn't realise that there was sufficient material on it to keep me occupied for months.

"Father," I worked up the courage to say, "if I'm breaking a rule by asking this please forgive me. Would it be possible to get a photo?"

He laughed, "Of course, as long as it's for personal use."

"Definitely," I promised, "I won't put it up on the internet or anything."

"Shall we take it out on the balcony?" He suggested.

I agreed, and while I was setting up the automatic timer he said "I have no problem with having my photograph taken, but what bothers me is when I catch visitors secretly taking a shot without asking. It makes me feel like an exhibit in a museum or an animal in a zoo." He laughed at the image and then we stood together for the shot.

As we said our goodbyes we embraced one another and rather sentimentally I said "Having time to talk with you has been the joy of my trip to Athos."

"It as been a joy for me to have you here," he responded generously.

I heard the solid wooden door closing behind me as I stepped into the courtyard. Above me on the balcony I could see the Russian priest deep in conversation with a monk. Knowing that I had the walk to Simonos Petra ahead of me I decided to gather my things and prepare to leave. As I was coming out from my room with my bag over my shoulder the Russian priest turned the corner and approached me.

"Father you are leaving?" He asked.

"Yes," I said and told him where I was heading.

"Simonos Petra is a wonderful monastery, the monks will make you most welcome."

We embraced and kissed each other's cheeks.

"Do you know who I should give my donation to for my stay?"

"Don't worry," he said, "just put it in the candle box in church."

I found the guestmaster and thanked him for the monastery's hospitality and then visited the church one last time. As I was pushing some folded notes through the slot of the donations box I realised that a monk was in the stall behind me. He was completely still except for his lips on which the movement of the Jesus Prayer kept time with the long black knotted rope which he slowly fed through his fingers. He made no response to my presence and so I quietly slipped out and eased the door shut as I left.

"Love is greater than prayer, because prayer is a particular virtue but love combines all virtues. Even a mother does not cling to the babe at her breast as a son of love clings to the Lord at all times."

- Saint John Climacus

Chapter Eleven

The path out of the monastery headed first towards the sea before climbing back up the mountainside and disappearing into the trees. I had been blessed with far more than I could have ever hoped for from my pilgrimage and I could have happily climbed on to a ferry and gone home. As I headed down towards the quay I noticed a young monk sitting alone on a wall. He looked up at me as I approached and through a friendly smile called out in Greek. I came to halt in front of him, my desire to keep moving and start my journey blinding me to the encounter that was taking place. When he heard that I was from England he said

"Please sit with me Father, I would like to talk if you have time."

I hesitated; the experience of getting lost had focussed me too much on my coming walk. My mind was already half a mile down the road. Seeing my uncertainty he stood and said "I will walk to the sea with you." He was a slight man which added to his youthful appearance. His thick accent was eastern European but I couldn't place it exactly.

"You are not Greek either?" I asked.

"No Father, I am from Romania. I have been on Athos for only six years."

"You must have been very young when you came here," I observed.

"Yes, although perhaps I am older than you imagine." It was true, the beards and asceticism made it hard to judge sometimes.

His face grew suddenly very serious. "Father, I want to speak to you about something."

We stopped walking and I wondered what he could have to say to a stranger that could be of such urgency.

"Father," he continued, "you must pray for the world."

This struck me as something quite ordinary and I nodded and assured him that I agreed.

"No Father, it is very important that you hear this message. The world must be prayed for, the whole world. There are terrible things coming and unless we pray it will catch us unprepared."

The more I talked with them the stronger the realisation grew that on Athos eschatology is never far from the conversation. I was in two minds. Perhaps this is the inevitable result of their lifestyle; after all, the writings of the early Church exhibit the same expectations and no one communicates a greater belief in a looming end of the world than Saint Paul. But as I listened to him I was impressed with the thought that this was more than a general spiritual state: his warning was motivated by a real concern and was clearly a response to the specific circumstances of our time.

"There is something happening in the world Father, you must be careful, watch carefully."

As much as I knew I should take him seriously his words did not affect me. I wasn't ready at that point in my plan for the day to engage with these thoughts.

When he paused I asked him if he could show me where I could fill up my bottles.

"I will take you there," he said, leading the way. "There is a tap behind the quay which has the coldest water of all."

We climbed a wooden staircase to a dimly lit hall that occupied the upper half of the building. A monk and two pilgrims were sitting at a long table, the seriousness of their conversation conveyed by their hushed voices. Through a door at the back of the room was a pipe that came out of the clay. I ran the water for a moment and was pleased to discover that the water was as cold as the monk had promised. I filled my bottles and tried to ease past the conversation taking place without causing too much disturbance. To my relief none of them even glanced my way and stepping outside I found the young monk now standing on a ledge that ran along the road I was about to take.

I confirmed that the water was good and thanked him for his help. He didn't smile at my attempt at pleasantries, but looked down at me with an added seriousness.

"Father, pray for the world, you'll see why soon enough."

This last comment sent a shiver through me, it caught me off guard and I stood motionless for a moment. We locked eyes and I could see he was watching for my reaction. I could think of nothing more to say than "Thank you, I will."

He told me his name and said that if I ever returned to Mount Athos I should ask for him. With that he wished me well and strode back up towards the monastery. I stood watching him for a little while, not really reflecting on anything, but taking in the effect of his warning. I was aware that I had been too closed off for the encounter to really go anywhere but knew that his words would stay with me.

I positioned my duffle bag into a comfortable position over my shoulder and began the climb. The first section of road was dusty but firm and wide enough for vehicles to use. I was pleased to discover that the skin on my legs had recovered and knowing that Simonos Petra was only ninety minutes walk away I was in good spirits. The sun was already beginning to bake me but I knew the path and I had a good supply of water.

After about twenty minutes or so I stopped to take my first drink. The path had not yet left the main road and I had completed the first uphill section. As I stood looking back at the view of Grigoriou I saw a white van kicking up a cloud of dust as it made its way up the hill towards me. I decided to wait until it had passed before resuming my journey so as to avoid breathing in the yellow fog in its trail. Through the windscreen I could see a layman driving with a white bearded monk in the passenger seat. As it got closer I smiled and waved. To my surprise it pulled up beside me and the monk wound down his window.

"Where are you going?" The monk asked.

When I told him he said "May I walk a little with you Father?"

"I would like that," I said.

"I will wait for you at the top of the hill."

With that the van pulled away and stopped about fifty metres ahead of me. The monk climbed out and the driver handed him a large bag which he placed on the ground. At that the van pulled away and the monk turned to watch me make my way towards him. I was already red in the face but far from exhausted. The path now went down into the trees and I was grateful for the shade.

He asked me the usual questions about where I was from and which monasteries I had visited. Then he said "Do you have time to have a drink with me?"

I could see a tap next to a large iron gate that prevented pilgrims from using a narrow path that went at a right angle to the one we were on. It seemed a good idea but instead of sitting by the tap he pulled a key out of his bag and unlocked the gate. Closing it behind me he led me down a steep path to a small white building that was hidden from view.

"This is my hermitage; I live here for eleven months of the year."

He unlocked the front door and waved me in ahead of him. The interior was simple but homely. A dark corridor led to two rooms. The first had a table and chairs at its centre, a few icons on the wall and nothing else.

"I will prepare a drink Father, but first please go through and venerate the icons."

He opened a door that led off to the second room which turned out to be a chapel. The iconostasis was covered in expertly painted images that were full of intense colours. I moved my way along the icons, venerating each in turn. This process left me calm and lifted from me the sense of movement and the physical exertion of the walk.

I went through to the room with the table and found him sitting in front of a tray of treats.

"Please Father, sit down and refresh yourself. Have you ever had a submarine?"

I wasn't familiar with the name and told him so.

His smile widened. He took a large spoon of pink goo from a jar and placed it in a glass of iced water. The goo stayed on the spoon.

"The water will cool it for you, please, enjoy." He waved his hand over the tray and I gratefully pulled out the spoon and took a mouthful. It was as refreshing as it sounded and he watched happily as I indulged myself. There was only one glass, one shot of apple spirit, and a full decanter of iced water. On a small plate was a pile of Turkish delight.

"Are you not having any Father?" I asked.

"No, no, please enjoy."

This spirit of hospitality on Athos was something I was becoming familiar with but this didn't reduce its impact on me. As I drank and ate he sat opposite me, his face full of warmth. Only on later reflection did I realise that the size of his bag probably meant he had been away from his hermitage for some time and yet his first priority had been to care for my needs. His face was one of complete acceptance. His eyes looked at me with a depth of love and care that I had never in my life seen before. The smile never left his face and as he looked at me it was as though he was not entertaining some priest from England but that he was being honoured with a visit from someone special.

"I did not see you at the Liturgy this morning. You should have let them know you wanted to concelebrate."

"I wasn't sure how I would be treated," I explained, "I had heard that some monasteries are wary of clergy from other places."

"You would have been welcomed," he said. "You are a priest regardless of where you are from. How did you become Orthodox in England?"

I gave a brief explanation and he listened intently.

"And is there anything that you are struggling with about Orthodoxy? Is there anything that you have found a problem?"

"No, nothing," I said, "in fact the more I have learned the more I realise how absolutely right everything is about it."

"Good, good," he nodded approvingly, "Orthodoxy is God's gift to us. It is not a religion like these other systems that men have created. It is revealed to us as a blessing, that we may know God. So many people are confused by all of these different teachings in the world; they imagine Orthodoxy is just one more path among many. It is good that you have found your home. We must do more to let people know about Orthodoxy, especially in England."

"Do you know England very well?" I asked.

"Oh yes, I visit Birmingham once each year. I hear confessions and help the priests there as much as I am able. There is a special quality to the English that I admire. I know your country has many problems, but still there is a nobility to be found there which is sadly rare in some places."

I was surprised to hear him say this, but learning that he was a priest I realised how easy it would be to confess everything to him. There was not a hint of judgement or condemnation in him, only loving acceptance. This was a priest to whom one could tell the most terrible of sins without fear. Without saying anything about it he was teaching me something very profound.

He then asked about my spiritual life and we talked at length about some of the most intimate parts of who I am and how I live. His love gave me a freedom to open myself up to his gaze. He imparted a confidence that enabled me to lower any barriers or attempts to conceal anything. After an hour or so I found myself seeing clearly things that had been submerged in emotion or confusion. His words were simple and full of clarity and the truth of his advice was instantly recognisable. He left me feeling that his only concern was my well being and I knew there was a healing property to his conversation that was filled with the Holy Spirit. Here was God's treasure, a living man whose presence could so powerfully carry other men into a deeper reality.

I finished the ice water and assured him that I didn't want more. Eventually we stood and walked through to the front door.

"Father, do you have a stick?" He asked.

"No, that's fine; it's not so far now."

"It is a steep climb, very difficult; you must take a walking stick."

He turned and reached into the shadows beside the door. He first pulled out a length of wood which had a smooth carved handle but beyond that was just a discarded piece of timber. It looked about the right length for me but before I could receive it he hesitated. He looked at it for a moment and put it back. He then revealed a carefully shaped stick that someone had taken great care over.

"Take this one," he instructed, "it is a good one."

"No, please Father," I protested, "I only need it for the walk to Simonos Petra, that's too good for my needs."

He thrust the stick into my hands and with a look as pleased as any parent on Christmas morning seemed satisfied that he had given me the best he could. I was embarrassed by his kindness.

"Thank you so much, and thank you for your hospitality."

"All of us here on Athos are guests of the Mother of God," he smiled, "whether you are here visiting for a week or staying for the rest of your life. This is her garden, she is our host." I nodded and smiled, convinced that he was right.

"Please lock the padlock on the chain at the gate Father," he said, "have a safe journey."

He stood at the door watching me walk away. Before I turned the corner and disappeared from sight we waved to one another and even from this distance I could see his face still illuminated with a smile.

"If a man have not the remembrance of death before him at all seasons, he will not be able to die to every man, and if he die not to every man he will be unable to be constantly before God."

- - Elder Macarius of the Desert.

Chapter Twelve

After leaving the hermitage the path descended for half an hour, twisting its way through the undergrowth and rocks. Every now and then there would be a glimpse of Simonos Petra high up on the cliff ahead. A lot of work had been devoted to keeping the path in good order. Planks had been inserted to prevent slippage and at no point anywhere was it in danger of succumbing to the advancing undergrowth. This created a sense of being in a controlled wilderness, a landscape that was both natural and guided by human hands.

I had now had a number of days with little more than a few hours sleep each night, my body had had enormous demands made of it, and yet I felt alert and energised. I began to reflect on where I was and the conversations I had shared. I knew being alone freed me from unnecessary chitchat and enabled me to experience everything without the added lens of someone else's perspective.

The path followed the walls of the valley, down one side and then up the other, the reverse of my previous day's route, and at the bottom I rested and enjoyed the view. I could see how the path climbed steeply along the cliff ahead of me and I realised how dangerous my descent had been. Before I set off again I heard voices from the trees and saw two pilgrims emerge, each carrying enormous rucksacks. They turned out to be Greek with no English. We spoke a few words in our respective tongues and accepting the inability to communicate beyond that they waved and continued on along the walk behind me.

The path ahead of me looked like it was made of irregular paving stones. It was a natural phenomenon but gave the impression of having been designed. Large boulders had been rolled to either side of the path that provided useful (and needed) places to sit when the lungs protested. The walking stick was proving to be of great benefit and made the steep climb a pleasure. And there were sections that really were a climb rather than a walk, it would have been easy to fall and roll all the way back down.

With plenty of rest stops it was another forty minutes or so before I saw Simonos Petra looming above me. It looked far more imposing from beneath and I began to imagine the pirates who had long ago climbed this hillside expecting to find great riches. As I got closer I began to hear the faint sound of bells. At first I could just make them out but as I drew nearer I could tell there was no pattern to their ringing but that they were definitely bells. I was a little confused by this as I had become accustomed to the beating of the symantron. Only when I reached a walled section of the path did the source of the sound reveal itself. Ahead of me, blocking my route, were six mules. Around their necks hung cowbells which chimed as they moved. One of the beasts was rolling in the dust, its four legs comically raised to the sky as it satisfied its urges, the bell being thrown from side to side as it moved. The heads of the others all turned to look at me as I came into sight and I wondered how they would react. Mules are an animal I had never encountered before and I wasn't sure of their temperament. As I got closer they continued to watch me without reaction. I knew I shouldn't shoo them out of the way in case they got spooked, but I didn't fancy pushing my way through them either. Instead I climbed the wall and balanced along it. Even with an Englishman tightrope-walking over them they remained placid and unmoved. There wasn't any visible vegetation around them and from close up I could see they weren't tied to anything. They were standing here, rolling in the sun, doing nothing except presumably waiting for water.

I jumped down on the other side of them and snapped a few photos to illustrate the story I would have to tell. Then off I continued, climbing towards the great edifice above. Nearer the monastery, but not yet amongst the buildings, the path was properly paved. Above it wooden frames had been constructed from which hung countless lemons. About twenty metres from the first of the stone structures was a tap. My water was now gone and I decided to replenish my bottles before going on. The water turned out to be hot. Not just warm, but properly hot. I drank from the tin cup and enjoyed the unusual sensation of hot water in the sunshine. It turned out to be much more refreshing than it sounds, but I decided to leave my water bottles until I found a different source. As I sat there a huge black and white butterfly fluttered towards me and settled on my arm. I slowly raised it to eye-level for inspection; it wasn't a variety I recognised. Alone on a hot mountainside I found the presence of this insect very comforting. Not that I was in any way unhappy, but the connection with another living creature felt good, far more than being close to the mules had been. Eventually it flew away to find whatever nameless flowers grew here, and I took it as a cue to set off again.

The outlying buildings of the monastery are two-storeys high and appeared to be made of the same grey stone as the paths. Tall red chimneys sprout from the roofs and everything looked clean and in good order. From my reading in preparation for the trip I knew that the monastery was dedicated to the Nativity of Christ. It was named after Simon the Athonite in the Thirteenth Century. It was known as the "New Bethlehem" because for two years he had seen a light shining over the ridge of the cliff where the monastery now stands. Positioned so precariously on the cliff I could understand why building work had been abandoned so often. When Simon's cell attendant had fallen to what was assumed to be his death, the discovery that he had miraculously survived gave courage to the workers to complete their task. The scaffolding which now clung to the side of the cliff looked no more technologically advanced than what had been used all those years ago and I pitied the soul whose work took him out over the ledge. A terrible fire had destroyed much of the structure in 1891 but Russian supporters had made sufficient donations to cover the repairs. Even with such relatively recent changes the monastery looked very ancient.

As I moved through the complex I saw that every doorway was arched and decorated, every wall included some kind of decorative design. Despite its great size, these features prevented the monastery from feeling austere or unwelcoming. Great care had been taken to insert coloured brick around the windows, ceilings were painted in two-tone, it was an environment of great beauty, an offering to God. But I assumed that it must also have a positive effect on the monks living there. Without ostentation they had created a homely environment even from stone.

A wooden sign pointed me to the guesthouse where I found a long dark table on which lay a visitors' register and a pen. I filled in my details and then looked back at the list of previous visitors. Almost all of them were Greek and the majority listed their occupation as "student". Like some cultural rite of passage the Greek men come to the

Holy Mountain in preparation for their adult lives. Perhaps to pray for guidance about their careers or maybe seeking help to find a good wife. All those concerns that young men carry are brought to the patient ear of God and the wise council of the monks.

A young Greek monk who spoke little English found me waiting and invited me through a set of large wooden doors to another waiting area. He asked me to sit and a few minutes later reappeared with the now familiar tray of treats. There was even more loukoumi than I was used to and a welcome shot of the apple-based spirit that cut through the dust of the road in my throat.

"I have the letter the monastery sent me," I said, reaching for my bag.

"No need Father," the monk said, waving his hand, "I will arrange your room, please wait here."

He left me to my treats and I sat admiring the large icons hung around the room. Just then two more pilgrims appeared in the doorway and I recognised them as the Italians I had met as I had walked from Xiropotamou. The mutual recognition led to smiles and they were suddenly emboldened to walk in and sit on the benches opposite me.

"How has your visit been going?" I asked.

"Very good Father, it is a very holy place."

I nodded my agreement. I discovered that the one had a reasonable grasp of English and the other used him as translator. I asked them about Italy and their background and could see they were a little hesitant to say too much about their faith: my black rassa made me look a lot more official than I felt. So I raised the topic of football and immediately they relaxed. I had watched a few games from the Italian league and threw in a few names of players and teams that I could recall. They became very animated at this and we jokingly disagreed about the merits of Paul Gascoigne.

It turned out they weren't staying at Simonos Petra but had come in looking for directions to Grigoriou. I was happy to oblige and moved to the doorway to point to the path they must follow. I repeated the warning I had received about the cliffs and told them where to find water. Before they set off I remembered the walking stick and retrieved it from the wall where I had propped it.

"Take this, it will be very useful."

Without hesitation the English speaking Italian took it and thanked me. He prodded the ground a few times with it as though testing it out and smiled with satisfaction that it was solid. As we were saying our goodbyes the guestmaster returned and asked me to follow him. We crossed a cobbled area to a two-storey building that looked newly built. The lower storey consisted of different shades of brick while the upper floor was cleanly white-washed. This was all punctuated with light brown timbers that softened its appearance and gave it the ook of a holiday-home.

We climbed a few steps and he led me along the corridor that ran down the middle of the building: on either side were six rooms. He pushed open one of the doors and we found a man in his early twenties sitting on one of the three beds. The monk said something in Greek and the young man quickly grabbed his belongings and stepped out of the room.

"Please Father," the monk gestured for me to enter. I realised that to accommodate a priest in the traditional manner, which is a room to himself, the previous occupant had been transferred. It was extremely humbling to be treated with such honour but I was relieved to have a quiet place to rest by myself.

"The veneration of the holy relics will begin in twenty minutes," he informed me. I checked my alarm clock, unpacked a few things, and then lay out on the bed. As in the other monasteries, everything was simple but extremely clean. The familiar slippers stuck out from under each bed and a large glass jug and tumbler had been provided. I gave myself ten minutes to relax and then found the washroom to freshen up. Other than a muted conversation I heard in one of the other rooms I didn't meet another soul and it felt like I had the place to myself. I had read that Simonos Petra is inundated with visitors during the summer months but the evidence so far convinced me that this was far from the case.

With five minutes to spare I pushed my money and passport under the mattress (even on Athos old habits are hard to shake) and crossed to the broad stone steps that let to a high archway. This was the entrance into the main monastery structure and once inside I discovered a labyrinth of sloping pathways which curved off to the left and right. At the top of the monastery the floor became a series of steps made of uneven stone that would be described as rustic in any other situation.

The door to the church was open and immediately I was confronted by huge frescoes of various saints. They stood ten feet high, and were obviously new as a few of them were only half finished. A heavy set of scaffolding indicated a work in progress. I moved through the first doorway to the second chamber where there were many framed icons and dark wooden stalls around the walls. A couple were occupied by monks in prayer who paid me no attention. Finally I made my way to the iconostasis where a priest was preparing the relics. He handled them with great reverence and even though I knew this was part of his daily routine he performed the task as though he were doing it for the first and only time.

I venerated some of the icons and found a stall to sit in while I waited for the service to begin. A half dozen other pilgrims arrived and stood in a semi-circle in front of the table. When I could see that the monk was about to start I joined them. He moved along the table identifying the relics and despite it being in Greek I recognised a few names. He repeated his explanation in English and in a state of awe I discovered I was kissing the relics of Saint John the Baptist, the Great Martyr Panteleimon, Martyrs Barbara and Eudocia, Saint Dionysius and many others. The monk took our prayer ropes from us and blessed them on the relics. As he returned mine to me I marvelled at what this little rope of knots already meant to me and knew the full impact of it having been blessed in such a way would only be discovered over time.

A small group of monks began to chant and it was apparent that the service of veneration was part of the community's routine and not just something laid on for pilgrims. After ten minutes or so of singing the monks moved to the relics and in turn venerated them just as the visitors had done. We then filed out and were led to the refectory. I was guided once again to a table near the abbot. The dishes of food were laid out before us as we stood and prayed the blessing. Once again I discovered the challenge of a whole cucumber was part of the meal. There were also plates of what looked like diced roast potatoes which were cooked in various herbs: they were delicious. It was at this meal I also discovered my love of tomatoes. They were as big as apples and after slicing them and mixing them into the dish I knew I had never tasted anything so fresh in my life.

There appeared to be more monks at Simonos Petra than at the other monasteries I had visited, and I was struck by how young so many of them were. A few could barely grow beards and yet had already responded to the monastic calling. Everyone ate in silence until a middle-aged monk began to read from a Greek text. The walls were painted with yet more large frescoes of saints and it was easy to sense ourselves surrounded by the heavenly hosts. There was no separation between eating and praying. On Athos men bring every activity before God and the angels and have a deep faith in the saints who pray alongside them.

At the end of the meal everyone stood and the customary blessing was given. We filed out in an orderly manner, row by row and I walked down the cool, narrow tunnels back to the hot sunshine. Outside I headed towards the wooden balcony that runs along the length of the guest house and found a shaded spot to sit and admire the view of the monastery. Dotted around on the hill were a number of sketes and hermitages. There was the usual stillness about them; the buildings sat silently while the great ascetic struggles went on inside.

I took out my prayer rope and began to say the Jesus Prayer. There was no distraction around or inside me. The stillness of Athos is a great aid to developing stillness within. I promised myself that when I returned to the world I would make time to escape the busyness of life and find somewhere to make this kind of space. Only when we taste it do we really understand how vital it is. But the paradox is that when we allow our time to become crowded with chores, with people and work, we are less able to perceive the damage this hectic lifestyle can have on us.

After a couple of hours I went back to my room. It was nearly ten o'clock and I wanted to catch up on my sleep. I placed the alarm clock on a chair next to the bed and was asleep within minutes. I had forgotten to push the switch over to set the alarm and for the first time during my trip I was woken by the symantron. I reached over and found I still had twenty minutes before the service began. I listened to the rhythms being tapped out and allowed my mind to take in the reality of the experience. It was my last night on Athos and I was keen to make the most of every moment.

I washed and dressed and in the cool night air responded to the call to prayer. In one of the corridors I met a tall white haired monk who slowly bowed to me before gliding on towards the church. The monks move without haste or rush, everything is controlled and steady.

A few monks had already gathered in church and trying not to trip over the long hem of my new rassa I venerated the icons. I was invited to a stall near the choir and despite my sleep was relieved to be able to sit. I bowed my head and looked for the stillness I had felt earlier. But there was no need to struggle for it, my mind was empty, the tiredness had caught up with me and I was incapable of entertaining any distractions.

In a stall near to mine I noticed a small monk who was extremely old and appeared to be blind. He was bent over, leaning on a short stick. He looked very frail and was the perfect image of the elder monk that I had created in my mind over the years. As the other monks entered the church a number stopped to hold his hand or gently squeeze his arm. This was done with such tenderness and love that I found myself quite moved. I saw a number of instances during the service where affectionate gestures and smiles were exchanged and I recognised how special the monastic bond was here.

The church itself was exquisite. The golden iconostasis was covered in beautifully executed icons. An enormous chandelier hung from the centre of the ceiling and other hanging lamps made the ascent and descent I had seen in Grigoriou but at a much more sedate speed. What was particularly striking at Simonos Petra though was the singing. The deep baritones which do not always sound so attractive on recordings now made their presence known. Without the intrusion of instruments the music made entirely by human voices was the closest I could imagine to heavenly choirs. The division between heaven and earth was dissolved and through the early morning hours I was carried in stillness to the heights of what mankind can do on earth. All of the art and technology of man's ingenuity were nothing compared with what the monks were offering to God. I was not only witnessing but was permitted to become a part of this offering and through it I knew I was seeing the possibility of change. In the most noble of human activities men are made noble. The true dignity of our humanity is glimpsed when we engage in the greatest of all human pursuits. When we seek to worship God we come closer to Him, the source of all our dignity, nobility and purpose.

The service moved quickly to the Divine Liturgy and I entered my final hour of prayer on Athos. I started to look at everything I could so as to retain as many memories as possible. It was then that I noticed a man who must have been there all night, dressed in a sports jacket and carrying an expensive looking camera. I knew photographs were prohibited in the churches but from where he had been placed by the monks it was obvious he was a guest of some importance. For some reason, his demeanour and clothing told me immediately that he was English.

When the service finished we each received a blessing from the abbot and gathered again in the refectory. Since the laymen are always seated at the rear of the hall I was curious to see the man from the church was seated at my table amongst the monks. It was amusing to see that he was unsure about the procedure for cutting up the food in front of us and when I heard him say "Thank you" to a monk handing him a jug of water I knew he was from my homeland. I was determined to speak to him at some point later and thought nothing more of it.

We filed out after breakfast and I decided to see as much of the monastery as I could before leaving. I followed one of the paths through a series of high arches and with no one in sight took a few photographs. I turned and was embarrassed to find a monk watching me. In broken English he advised me to go further along the path and pointed to a gate. I assumed he was telling me where to find the best shots but as I passed through the gate I found myself in the monastery graveyard.

There were less than twenty graves in a small area of neatly trimmed grass. The inscriptions on the crosses were in Greek but I could see that one of them was for a particularly important monk from the large carved stone on his grave. The custom is for the bodies to be exhumed after a few years and the bones stored amongst the dried remains of previous generations of the community. Standing amongst the graves I realised that the monk had not only been directing me to somewhere of interest or photographic value, but he was definitely relaying a message. I put my camera away and thought about more appropriate things.

The graves marked the stopping off point between this world and Resurrection and it was easy to contemplate issues of mortality surrounded by the signs of our inevitable future. I decided to head back and as I came out through the gate I spotted the Englishman coming down the path towards me. I approached him and in the thickest Greek accent I could imitate I said

"You are English, yes?"

He politely smiled and in an upper class accent confirmed his nationality.

"I like England," I continued. "I like to visit England. I come stay with you, yes? You give me your address and I come stay with you."

What little colour there was in his face now drained instantly. He became flustered and didn't know how to respond. It was a horrible idea to have me turn up on his door but being on Athos he clearly didn't want to be inhospitable. When he looked as uncomfortable as he could possible be, I burst out laughing,

"It's alright," I said in my usual voice, "I'm English too."

His laughter was more from relief than enjoyment of the joke, "You certainly don't look English."

"What has brought you to Athos?" I asked.

"I'm working with World Heritage, I'm an architect by trade and I'm giving a talk in Athens next week and it seemed sensible that I should have at least seen in the flesh some of the things I'm going to be discussing."

We chatted a little about our respective impressions of Simonos Petra and agreed on how blessed we were to be visiting. He turned out to be Anglican and said he'd never experienced Orthodox worship before: he conveyed the deep impression it had made on him.

He was returning to the world that day like myself and told me about a mini-bus that had been arranged to take him to Daphne. He kindly offered me a lift which meant I had two hours before I had to leave.

"Just because I cannot drink the whole river does not mean I cannot take water from it in moderation for my needs."

- Saint Cyril of Jerusalem

Chapter Thirteen

I retrieved my things from the room and decided to sit in the open area outside the main entrance to the monastery. This way I thought I would be able to see the bus if it tried to leave without me but also I would have a chance to watch the comings and goings of monks and pilgrims.

There was a wooden bench laid across a low wall on which I dropped my bag and made myself comfortable. I had a good view of both the sea and the monastery and knowing I would be leaving soon I tried to make the scene a permanent picture in my mind. Just then I heard the familiar sound of cow bells and looking up the hill spotted the mules from the previous day. This time they looked very different. They were tied in line following in single file behind an old monk as he headed off into the mountains. Every one of the animals was carrying a full load as they stoically marched up the path. It was a scene that could have come from any point in the last thousand years.

While my attention was on the mules a monk and a pilgrim came out of the monastery and sat near to me on the wall. I wished them a good morning in one of the few Greek phrases I had at my disposal and then apologetically had to explain why I couldn't understand when the monk began speaking quickly to me. He turned out not to have any English at all but the layman had enough that we could relay a few basic messages between us. My lack of understanding enabled them to converse freely without being concerned about me overhearing and from the way they spoke I could see they were discussing something serious. The sound of their voices brought me back to reality and I thought for the first time in what seemed a long time about returning to England. It then occurred to me that I had the name of a monk at Simonos Petra with me. The father of one of my Greek parishioners had once visited us and in conversation had told me that he had once been the chairman of an organisation called "The Friends Of Mount Athos". Hearing that I was planning a pilgrimage he had written the names on the back of his business card of monks who could speak English and who he thought would be happy to meet with me. I had brought it with me but forgotten to use it. I took out the various pieces of paper that were stuffed in my pocket and there was his card. When there was a lull in the conversation beside me I asked if the monk knew of Father "A". The layman translated and the monk's message came back as positive.

"He says would you like for him to go and fetch Father "A"?"

"Yes please," I confirmed, hoping I wasn't imposing on them.

The monk nodded and flitted off into the building. I made a little conversation with the layman and discovered he was catching the ferry that morning to stay at the Monastery of Karakalou which was on the opposite side of the peninsula. I realised that my plan to visit monasteries closely grouped around Daphne had looked good on paper, and the walking had been manageable, but was not really necessary. There is a reliable and regular ferry service that runs around the coastline each morning making access to all of the monasteries there very easy. I was already making mental notes for a future trip.

The monk returned with Father "A". He was a tall thin man with a full greying beard and a face that had been sculpted by years of fasting.

"Hello Father," he said with a pleasant Greek accent.

I explained how I had got his name and that I hoped he didn't mind. Whether it was the mention of my Greek friend or that he generally was happy to meet pilgrims I couldn't tell, but to my relief he made it clear that I was welcome to some of his time. The other monk and pilgrim had gone back into the monastery building leaving us alone in the open air.

"You are from England Father?" He asked.

"Yes, this is my first visit to Greece."

"It is good that you are Orthodox in England, you must thank God for this. It is a place deeply affected by the Reformation."

I nodded agreement, "I used to be Anglican, it is going through a difficult time."

"It is not just a difficult time now, do you mean the church or the country?" He asked.

"I meant the Church of England."

"Oh yes, the people of England were robbed of their faith. The Norman invasion was blessed by the pope to spread Roman Catholicism in England, which is why you have so many Norman churches even today. They divided the country up into parishes and implanted their religion on an Orthodox people. This was your nation's first tragedy and from there it was lost. The Reformation was motivated by good intentions for sure, Luther was seeking the truth, but he could only see the Roman Church and did not understand the full picture. His rejection of Roman abuses was not wrong, but he didn't know that Rome had already split from the true Church in 1054. And so he thought to create a church from scratch which is impossible. They had no links with the traditions of the Apostles and the Early Church which were still alive in Orthodoxy. They replaced the pope with the Bible and thought they were free to interpret it how they would. Every Protestant has become his own pope because he believes his will and reading of Holy Scripture is final." He shook his head, as though hearing these things himself for the first time. "But Luther was far from the worse," he continued. "In Switzerland the followers of Zwingli protested by eating sausage in Lent. This was the level of their thinking, to oppose anything they thought was not in the Bible by degrading it. They had no idea that it was the Church that decided on the canon of the New Testament in the late three hundreds. What did they think was going on for three hundred years? And who do they think were the men who gave them their Bible? It was the very bishops of the Church that they thought they were now rejecting. But it is not true. They were protesting against Roman clergy who had themselves been separated from the Church for half a millennium."

"This is not the version of history that is taught in England," I said.

"No, of course, and the poor people of England are not to be judged. They are denied the sacraments and yet still manage to produce some holy people. God is generous and merciful and does not forget us even when we stray far from His vineyard. Our Lord taught us the parable of the sheep that was lost, do you understand this story?"

"Yes, I think so."

"The lost sheep is really the whole of humanity," he explained, "Christ came to earth as our Shepherd to find us and take us home. The other ninety-nine are the angels. God wants for us to return infinitely more than we could ever want it ourselves and this is why we may be saved." He paused and crossed himself in gratitude.

168

"There are many devout people in the Church of England," I said.

"Yes, of course," he smiled. "There are good people to be found in every religion. There are good Jews and Muslims and Hindus. But this is not enough. What we think is good is far from God's perfection. So long as we are sinful we will be alien to God's nature. This is why we must repent and repent again. We must slough off those parts of ourselves that prevent us from union with God. And ultimately only God can make us perfect. The Holy Spirit is the One who purifies us; it is not achievable through our own efforts in being good."

"But don't you see evidence that the Holy Spirit is working in people outside the Church?" I asked.

"Of course, God's life and goodness have been poured out to the four corners of the universe and continue to be poured out. God does not abandon His creatures: life would be unbearable if we did not have God's goodness. But there is a difference between this and the specific help God gives through His Church. God has called us into relationship with Him and chooses to bless us in very specific ways. Christ told us that if we do not eat His Body and drink His Blood we do not have His life in us. God's will is that we share in His life and receive His grace within the Body of Christ. There is order not chaos. We are called to share in Him with each other. Our bond is with each other just as it is with God. The Protestant reformers introduced a spiritualised understanding of Holy Communion which they didn't realise was really the old Gnosticism that the Church had defended the truth against many centuries before."

These words struck me very deeply and I understood why he was willing to share his time with me. I was not just a random stranger from another land, he was living out his belief that we were united, mystically joined as part of Christ's Body.

"I'm at a loss as to what to say to people back in England," I said.

"It is not your responsibility to change everything, don't let your pride lead you into such ideas. But you must demonstrate your faith in the way you live, try to love your neighbour, do all the things Christ commanded us to do. This is enough. There are many good things even about the Anglican Church but I am afraid it has changed beyond recognition in recent years. I was once part of a group that held discussions with Anglican theologians. We looked for common ground in the hope of bringing England back. But England's church has cut itself off from authentic Christianity. It has ordained women, it has accepted worldly morality, there are same-sex relationships blessed in its churches. I no longer participate in these talks because there is no longer any point. The Church of England has gone the way of so many Protestant groups. But we should not be surprised by this. Schism only leads to schism. All we can pray for now is that individuals and sometimes groups will find their way to Orthodoxy."

I felt very sad hearing these things. It wasn't a situation I wanted to accept, but I knew it was true. I let out a short sigh as I resigned myself to the reality of the mess my country was in.

"Don't be downhearted by this." He was smiling again. "Put your trust in the love of God, you can do no more. Ultimately all things are in God's hands, we must have faith that all will be as it should. So often our fear and anxiety comes from our not wanting to face our struggles. But the saints tell us that when we endure, when we are faithful in our sorrows God does not turn away from us. Remember Christ's words about the sparrows and even the flowers in the fields. How much more is each of us to God. We are loved beyond our imagining and yet our hearts are often full of resentment and anger. This is the devil's work who wants us to be miserable. We should resist the temptation to be downhearted because it is destructive and comes from evil."

Once again he crossed himself and it was at this point that I noticed the prayer rope that he was running though his fingers. Even as he spoke to me he was praying the Jesus Prayer. I knew he was praying for me and wanted to ask about it but thought better of it. Instead I raised the issue that had cropped up time and again.

"Father, a number of monks have said things to me about the coming difficulties that the world is to face. What do you think about this?"

His face was full of compassion as he looked at me, "I have no special insight into these things. But none is needed. Too many people get excited about prophecies and signs. I know a hermit who refuses to see any pilgrims because he was asked constantly for healings or secrets about the end of the world. This is not the way we should live as Christians. Yes, Christ told us to look out for the signs, and we must be ready for whatever is to come. But really we should try to be Christian, this is enough. I tell visitors that they should seek to do the ordinary things: fast, say their prayers, try not to sin too much, repent when they fall, go to church regularly, receive the sacraments. These are the things that are needful. Not enough people are doing these things today. Do you think it would cause a scandal or be recorded in the history books if someone ate sausage in Lent today? Of course not because too few people care anymore. This is the real danger around us. Anti-Christ will come when he will, but before then people are letting go of the traditions of the Church that the Holy Spirit has taught us. How can we ever hope to face martyrdom if we cannot even resist a piece of meat on Friday? Self-discipline, self-control in little things should be our goal. The Christian life is not easy, it makes demands on us, we should try to be ordinary Christians before we fantasise about higher things. You must go back to your parish and serve the Liturgy. Try to love the people God has given to your care. Don't worry when things go wrong or you face difficulties. The devil will try to trip you, and God will test you. But so long as you do what is required you are doing enough. God will bless you if you are faithful and Orthodoxy will be available to English people once again."

I felt grounded by this advice. We talked for another thirty minutes or so and then the English architect appeared with an expensive looking leather travel bag. He waved and came over to us. I introduced them and the monk asked a few questions about his work and what he hoped to achieve on Athos. It was clear from his responses that though he had come to examine stone work the living stones had had a profound effect on him. As they spoke a mini-bus pulled up alongside us, a tired looking monk at the wheel. He climbed out and shouted something in Greek to us. Father "A" translated for us, "He says he will be leaving in ten minutes." At this we all stood and I thanked him for his words.

"Don't let the world take your peace from you," was his parting comment and with that he turned and returned to his cell.

After so much time feeling like a foreigner it was good chatting with another Englishman and I was keen to hear more about the world heritage status of Athos.

"Did they send you because you have a connection with the Orthodox?" I asked.

"No no," he said. "It is purely because of my work experience."

"What have you made of Orthodoxy?"

"I have visited a number of Orthodox churches in other parts of Greece, but Athos is something else."

I agreed and asked what might have been an abrupt question under other circumstances.

"Are you happy with Anglicanism?"

"Well, of course there are things we are struggling with. My wife and I belong to an Anglo-catholic parish but one cannot escape what is happening in the wider communion."

"Do you think you will remain Anglican?"

"I think so; it has been our tradition for so long now I don't think we could feel comfortable elsewhere." He smiled and added "I suppose every denomination has its problems. That's what comes from being imperfect people."

I didn't object to this statement, but I knew it came from a dissatisfied man.

After a few more minutes the driver reappeared and gruffly told us to get in. Another monk sat in the front with him, but we two Englishmen had the rest of the bus to ourselves. The monk slid the door shut and turned the ignition of what sounded like an engine in its last few years of life. There were no seatbelts in the back seats but I was to discover these would have been of little use had the worst happened.

The bus pulled away and I allowed myself to look back at the monastery one last time. We took the same route I had walked, except for my special short cut, and I was interested to see how long it would take riding. However, such calculations quickly left my mind as I became preoccupied with the speed we were travelling. Our driver seemed oblivious to the cliffs and as we hurtled round single track dusty roads the image of us rolling over the edge filled me with real fear. There were no barriers of any kind and the surface consisted of compacted dust. I hadn't checked the condition of the tyres before we got in but I was guessing from the sound of the engine that they wouldn't be completely road-worthy: not that we had a road to drive on.

I looked at my fellow passenger and saw a look of terror in his eyes. We made no attempt to conceal our fear from one another as we willed the vehicle to stay on the track.

"Thank goodness we're going this direction," he said through tightened lips. "If we meet another van we'll be pulling in to the mountain and they'll have to go into the sea."

There was no humour in his comment, he was making a judgement of our likelihood of survival and I was grateful for even this worthless bit of information to cling to. We were taking blind corners at forty miles an hour or more and the slightest skid would have killed us all. I tried to pray but the truth is my mind had turned to jelly and I was just gripping my seat trying to stay calm. I kept telling myself that the roads would be familiar to the driver, he'd probably made this journey many times before, and I'd never heard of anyone actually driving off an Athonite cliff. Maybe the driver's faith was just that much stronger than ours, but I promised myself that if I ever returned to the Holy Mountain I would never accept a ride with a monk again.

After about fifteen minutes I spotted Daphne up ahead along the coast and began to have hope that we would make it. Mercifully we met no other vehicles and throwing up a cloud of dust all the way we eventually pulled in beside a few other cars behind the shops at the quay. My fellow passenger's face was now free of panic and we nervously smiled at oneanother. He slid back the door and jumped out. I lent forward and asked the driver if I could make a contribution towards the cost of the petrol. He strongly protested and I thanked him for the lift. Relieved to have survived I jumped through the open door and realised that the road between Daphne and Simonos Petra had threatened to snuff me out in both directions. Now that I was safe I found it amusing, but I still clung to the promise I had made to myself that next time I'd be riding the ferry.

The Englishman was waiting for me at the front of the van. As I came round to him he extended his arm to shake my hand; I knew I would forever be a part of his memory of that journey just as he would be in mine. We wished each other well and I headed towards the port office. An open door revealed a large room where about a dozen men were sitting on the bench that ran along the walls. Approaching two younger members of the group I asked if they spoke English and was pleased to discover they were fluent.

"Where do I buy my tickets for the ferry?" I asked.

"Round there," said the one, pointing back through the door and to the right. I thanked him and went in the direction he had indicated. A tall pilgrim stood waiting outside an open window and I presumed this was the ticket counter, but there was no sign of any sort to indicate this. After a short while a heavy middle-aged man appeared looking very flustered and hot. I heard the man in front of me say "Ouranopolis" and knew I was in the right place. I had pre-booked my seat on the ferry and quoted the number to the man selling tickets. He muttered the price and then slid the ticket towards me.

"How long before the ferry leaves?" I asked.

"Forty minutes," he said before disappearing back into his office.

I had time for a little shopping and decided to pick up a few gifts. There were now quite a few men hanging around and I had read that leaving Athos can be like crossing the border from one country to another. The Friends of Mount Athos warn on their website that this can be quite thorough because there is concern about visitors stealing priceless icons or other artefacts from the monasteries. Judging from the crowd that was gathering I thought it would be sensible to give myself plenty of time to go through this process so I didn't hang around too long doing my shopping. The young shopkeeper who had been keen to sell me the rassa came over and loudly announced how happy he was to see me again. I didn't think he hoped to make another big sale and presumed his greeting must have been genuine. He asked about the monasteries I had visited and then told me to choose something nice from his shelves.

There was an excellent stock of icons, both printed and hand painted, but the latter were beyond my price range. A familiar image of the Theotokos standing over the peninsula took my eye, and along with a couple of prayer ropes for my sons and a little incense, I came out with a bag not costing very much but which I was pleased with.

Concern about passing through the inspection process of the port authorities then prompted me to go back to the large waiting room. There were fewer people waiting now and I took this as a sign that things were happening. I joined what I thought was the end of the queue and began my wait.

Over the next twenty minutes more men joined us, some wandering in and sitting where they liked, others trying to work out where they should be in the queue. As the room began to fill there developed a sense of chaos and it was quickly becoming impossible to establish the correct order for when the officials would call us through. One or two men began leaning over the counter to see what was happening but as time moved on, no one was invited forwards. We had all seen the last person to go through having his bag checked; it had taken at least five minutes with some serious questioning going on. As I looked around I realised that there wouldn't be time for everyone to be processed in time for the ferry and it was clear that the rest of the crowd was becoming equally impatient. I felt exasperated at the lack of organisation in the place and was ashamed to catch myself thinking "We would never do it like this in England!"

Eventually through the large windows we could see the ferry approaching with about ten minutes before it was due to set off again. We watched helplessly as it docked and the crowd of new pilgrims alighted to begin their exploration of Athos. When the last man was off one of the port officials opened a door next to the counter and shouted something in Greek. Suddenly everyone rushed forwards and tried to get through the door and I realised that no one's bags were being checked, it had become a free-for-all to get onto the ferry. I climbed to my feet and joined the mass of bodies pressing towards the bottle neck of one small door in a large room of energetic Greeks.

The flow became quite rapid and pretty soon I was standing in line in the sunshine waiting to board the boat. One of the crew was checking both ferry tickets and diamonitirions and I wondered how they would react if someone had outstayed their permitted time. Once on board I walked the length of the ship and climbed the stairs to the shaded roof where I had enjoyed such good views on the trip coming out. There were fewer passengers this time and after a brief pause the ferry began its slow reverse away from the quay. Daphne quickly became part of the view and unlike my condition just a few days before I now lost all sense of reserve and took out my camera to snap shots of everything I could see. Notions of what was the proper way to act or whether I was behaving like a tourist were now irrelevant to me: I simply didn't care how I appeared to other people.

Returning to my seat I found a young monk sitting opposite me who looked like he'd swapped his clothes for rags. His head was bowed and he ran a long rope of knots through his hands. He stayed like this for most of the trip and his presence was one of great humility. One of the lessons from Athos is that it is sometimes enough to see and be around prayerful people. We do not always have to be taught in words; in fact the things we say may often be the least effective means of communicating important truths. The way we live, even the way we carry ourselves, can convey the reality of what we are and what we believe.

The monasteries along the coast no longer looked like the impressive historical structures I had seen before. I now had a small sense of the life within them and as we passed each one I could only think of the monks within the walls. I had only been on Athos for four days but if I was honest with myself I wasn't sure if I could have coped with being there much longer. I needed sleep and I needed to relax, but there was more to it than that. The experiences had been of such intensity and I had been so alert the entire time that I needed to shut down for a little while to take it all in. I was simultaneously drained and filled in different ways.

As Ouranopolis came into sight I realised that the mountains of Athos are visible from the little town.

As we returned to the world the peak of Athos was a distant point of rock shrouded in the haze of mist and cloud. It had already become a distant place again, and the familiar shapes of cars and hotels were rushing towards us.

A small group of wives was waiting to greet the ferry and it was an odd sensation to be seeing women again. They looked very different to the all-male world I had so quickly grown accustomed to living in and I had a strong desire to be with my wife again. For some of us the monastic experience can only ever be in the context of a pilgrimage, I knew in my heart that God had called me to be both a priest and a husband.

"Fragile is earthly happiness, and blessed is the man who does not chase after it, but places all his hope in Christ the Saviour – he shall not be put to shame."

- Elder Barsanuphius of Optina.

Chapter Fourteen

From the ferry I headed straight to the pastry shop that was part of a café in Ouranopolis' square next to the tower. I then carried my lunch to the beach, threw down my bag and consumed the meat dish with delight. Along the beach there were families sunning themselves and a few braver souls paddled in the waves. I could still see the peak of Athos reminding me of everything I had seen.

Eventually I made my way along the sea front and was offered a room in the same hotel as on my first night. It was a double room with air conditioning and a large flat screen television. There was a little balcony that overlooked a quiet backstreet which I knew I would be coming back to before the day was done. I went out and purchased a few cans of beer, left them in the room's mini-fridge, and took a hot shower which was long overdue. Stretched out on the bed with a beer in my hand I casually flicked the T.V. channels and found one broadcasting exclusively Orthodox items. I watched a priest in a studio arguing with a young man, and though it was in Greek without subtitles I happily absorbed the spectacle. In this state I fell to sleep for a while and when I woke the sky was still bright but it hinted at the change of day to evening.

I dressed and wandered down to the open air restaurant situated on the edge of beach. There were only a couple of tables busy and the barman was happy to chat at the bar. He told me he was Romanian and that he and his girlfriend had been working in Greece for nearly a year. They rented a room from their employer and he seemed happy with the situation.

After a couple of cold beers I took a walk along the bar front and noticed how civilised everything seemed. There were no crowds of rowdy youths that would inevitably gather if this was England and as the night drew in I felt completely safe strolling around. Eventually I headed back to my room and sat on the balcony to finish my other can of beer. The television was tuned to traditional Greek music and as I sat looking up at the stars an immense gratitude swept over me. Not just for the relaxing scene in which I found myself but for how blessed I had been on my pilgrimage. I couldn't have hoped for half of what had happened, the journey had felt very complete, I was left without any regret over any unfulfilled ambitions.

Despite my earlier nap, and no doubt in part due to the beer, I got to bed early and slept deeply. I woke before the alarm clock went off and had time for another shower. I went down to breakfast and helped myself at the buffet. As I was eating the Russian woman brought me a plate of pasta with a simple tomato sauce that was delicious. A couple and their young daughter joined me in the restaurant and before eating they sang their prayers. It was touching to hear the pre-school aged child joining in, her little voice keeping time with her parents.

I gathered my things, paid my bill and headed back towards the centre of Ouranopolis. I had decided to catch the later bus so as to give myself time to do a little shopping. As I walked through the early morning shoppers an old woman approached me and pushed what I guessed were her two grandchildren towards me. Following her instructions they each held out their hands for a blessing. I happily obliged and all three then kissed my hand. It was a moving moment and one that didn't raise any eyebrows amongst the people passing by.

Ouranopolis has many shops catering for the pockets of pilgrims. There are icons for sale everywhere, in chemists, supermarkets, where ever shoppers might turn there is the chance to purchase a holy image. It feels a little tacky at times but a few still caught my eye. I found myself standing in front of a church outfitters store. The window was full of vestments and thurables as well as some stunning hand painted icons which were enough to get me through the door. I had very little money left but was content to look around. The woman behind the counter enquired if she could be of help (at least I guessed that's what she asked) and I told her I was fine.

"You are English?" she asked excitedly.

"Yes," I admitted.

"You are the first English Orthodox priest I have had in my shop. Please Father, a blessing."

In the space of less than ten minutes I found myself giving a second blessing and suddenly felt guilty for not having much cash to splash around. I picked out a couple of inexpensive items so as not to leave empty handed. As I took them to the till the woman came round to me again.

"Please Father, take these for your parish in England." She pushed a box of charcoals and a bag of rose incense into my hand. I expressed my thanks and paid for the other items.

Outside I checked the time and decided to hang around in the square for the forty minutes until the next bus was due. I bought another pastry and planted myself on a bench where I could watch for the bus but also enjoy the flow of people coming and going around the shops. As I sat there a car pulled up and the driver jumped out and trotted towards me. After first trying to speak to me in what sounded like decent Greek when I told him I was English he looked pleased.

"That works better for me, Father, I'm Canadian. Can you point me to the Pilgrim's Office for Athos?"

"Do you have a reservation?" I asked.

"No," he said, "do I need one?"

His face dropped slightly when I told him I thought he did, but still he drove off in the direction I described in the hope I was wrong.

The bus arrived a few minutes later than scheduled and the driver got out and locked the bus behind him. Ten minutes later he reappeared and passengers gathered from around the square to climb aboard. I showed him my return ticket and found myself a dusty seat near the back. It was a different driver to my last trip and so I didn't try to ask about a lost rassa. The bus was about half full when we eventually pulled away and feeling infinitely more relaxed than when I had last made the trip down this road we headed towards Thessalonica.

At the bus station I tried to ask if there was any system for enquiring about lost property but I was met with blank stares. It wasn't a surprise so I shrugged it off and walked out to the taxi rank. The middle-aged driver of one of the taxis signalled for me to use his car which I was willing to do. He couldn't speak a word of English but assured me that he knew my hotel. He was true to his word, and after fifteen minutes of snaking through duel-carriageway traffic we pulled up outside a very plush looking establishment. He charged me very little for the ride and I entered the foyer to find a smart looking young man who welcomed me with an air of professionalism that was very reassuring. He took my details handed me a key and I took the lift down to the lower floor. I had opted to save money with the cheapest room available and wondered what my money would be buying. But there was no need to be anxious, the rooms were as plush as the rest of the hotel and I was in for a night of luxury.

I bought a bottle of beer at the bar and went out to the pool. This turned out to be a mistake as I found myself surrounded by people in swimsuits looking very uncomfortable to have a priest in their midst. The waiter brought out a bowl of crisps (chips as he called them in the American fashion) and I consumed them as quickly as I could. I swallowed the beer quickly to have an excuse to return indoors and took a stool at the bar. Above the shelves of bottles was a huge television screen and it was permanently tuned to a news channel with English subtitles. The reporters were relaying stories of war in Syria and my mood was quickly changed by the images of fighting. As the report switched back to the studio it was revealed that the American President was wanting to bomb Syria. Even as I heard this news the words of the monk walking beside me at the Monastery of Grigoriou came back to me.

Surrounded by leather seats and rich dark wooden tables, drinking beer and hearing the splash of a hotel swimming pool, the reality of the world felt dangerously close. We were playing in our luxurious setting while people suffered and died and politicians argued for war. I realised that I had fallen back into a worldly state of mind within moments of coming to land after Athos. I felt ashamed to be sitting there pretending everything was okay, that it was reasonable to be living like this while people's lives were falling apart. If Christ had returned at that moment how could I have accounted for myself? I remembered the parable of the rich man who ignored Lazarus at his gates and knew exactly which of the characters represented me.

The following morning the owner of the hotel gave me a lift to the airport and we chatted about the state of the economy. He painted a sad picture with little hope for the nation, especially for those under twenty-five. There was a lot of anger in his words and I knew there was the potential for real upheaval in a country where ordinary people are left with so much resentment towards a political class that is deaf to their cries. One word repeatedly on his lips was "bankers".

At Thessalonica airport I had the best part of an hour to sit and watch the crowd. The call for my flight appeared on the electronic panel and I joined the queue at the gate. The same buses carried us out to the aeroplane and pretty soon I was seated and ready for England. I took out a book written by the abbot of Grigoriou explaining The Lord's Prayer and before I knew it the flight was nearly over. I watched the shapes of fields pass beneath us as we approached Gatwick and I could see the familiar grey sky of home.

A couple of train rides later and I was sitting in the cold of Newport station in Wales waiting for my final connection. I could see lush green hills that were unmatched anywhere I had been for their rich, fertile soil. As I headed towards my platform a group of teenagers shouted abuse across the rails at me. They were mimicking what must have sounded to them like the sound of foreign tongues. I was tempted to call back in the most English voice I could summon up but then realised that an English accent might not be the best response in the Welsh Valleys. I looked at them with nothing to say; knowing that this was not my home, that we spoke the same language, but that I really was a stranger in this land.

To see the photographs taken on this journey search for "*Mount Athos Father Spyridon*" on Youtube.

Lightning Source UK Ltd.
Milton Keynes UK
UKHW040634140820
368251UK00001B/286